MW01174548

cheap NEWSLETTER... of only MONSTER films

a bi-weekly publication for MONSTER movie lovers worldwide....

MONSTER will be my "fun" 'zine. I also edit and publish another one called VIDEO*VOICE. That is more of a serious 'zine. It's a full size, offset, twenty-four page 'zine which takes up a lot of my time, and doing it is an incredible brain drain! So, I decided to write a bi-weekly 'zine dedicated to the ultimate film genre: the monster movie! While V*V will be my serious 'zine, MONSTER will be more of a laid-back, "what the hell" type of publication. Don't knock it if it only costs 35¢! I'm even offering Subscription rates ( which V*V doesn't offer ). With this introduction now outa the way, I'll get down to the reviewing stuff. One other thing that makes this one-pager different from V*V is that I'll be looking at stuff that is in the theatres as well as in the video stores ( V*V only looks at videos ).

## Volume One * Issue One

35¢

### December 5th, 1988

CHILD'S PLAY
You'll wish it was only make-believe.

BRAIN BLOOD

CHILD'S PLAY is a good film, but nowhere near the terrifying classic that I've heard some speak of it as. Clearly, the automation with Chuckie is a wonder to behold, and every bit of praise should be given to those hard-working people who constructed the killer doll. The story deserves a slap on the back for some originality, though I have seen better variations on the evil doll theme ( i.e. DEAD OF NIGHT — the all time classic ). Tom Holland, who crafted the frightfully funny vampire film FRIGHT NIGHT, has a tight hold on the reigns of directorship, nonetheless I thought he could have coaxed some better acting out of the material he had to work with ( though the kid was wonderful ). The plot: a savage killer is chased into a toy store by a cop. There, once fatally wounded, he sprawls dying at the base of a Good Buddy toy display. Summoning up the powers of a long forgotten god he transfers his soul into the doll with a thunderous explosion of mystical-psyonic energies ( one wonders at this point why he didn't annihilate the cop as easily as he totally blew up a toy store ). A day later a mother buys the very same doll from a peddler that happened to get it out of the wrecked store...from there Chuckie takes his revenge on his wimpy partner in crime, the cop who shot him in his previous existance and whoever gets in his way. The film actually worked up some wonderful suspense for me which I hadn't experienced since I saw ALIENS a few years back ( not to say CP was as good as it was different ). A few minor bits of the film bothered me though. Holland may be making a statement against toy-TV tie ins ( G.I. JOE, TRANSFORMERS, etc. ), but what I think he may be hinting at is the way adults treat kids. Sure, adults devise those absurd TV shows just to have the kids buy their products. But then those very same adult refuse to believe in the very same kids whom they love and apparently ( though falsely ) understand. That is frightening, not the film itself. A bit: so what happens to the child at the end of the film? By all rights he should be locked up as insane ( along with all of those who saw Chuckie and insist the thing was alive ). All evidence points to his killing at least three people ( fingerprints. ). At least the doll is destroyed and we don't have a sequel hinted at. You can thank some intelligence on Holland's part for killing that threat off. All in all, CP is a good, tense, and fun shocker.... where the MONSTERS are both the doll and the adults.

# EDITORIAL:

Lo and behold the first issue of *MONSTER!* as it stands today. Originally, *MONSTER!* was a quasi-stream-of-consciousness 'zine and companion publication to *Video Voice* and *NAKED!SCREAMING!TERROR!* (my other Kronos Productions I published with David Todarello). *MONSTER!* was my knee-jerk publication reaction to all the slasher films that were tumbling out of Hollywood, the Indies, and from around the world. Monsters have always been my first love, and I was determined (in my own way) to keep the genre alive.

Issue One was a single-page paste-up consisting of newspaper clippings, Xerox bits and pieces, and lots of cheap transparent (now yellowed) tape. The text and logo were created on my old (then still newish) MacPlus and printed on a dot-matrix printer. Then, as now, my love of dense text blocks was evident as I was into a small, compact-font text sizes.

Back then, prior to the explosion of the Internet in the '90s, 'blogs in the 2000s, and streaming information in the 2010s, *MONSTER!* was discovered by word of mouth, reviews in fellow 'zines and Mike Gunderloy's (sadly forgotten) monthly info-catalog, *Factsheet Five*. To my surprise, *MONSTER!* began to catch on and grew from a bi-weekly one-sheeter to a small digest-size 'zine that we moved to a monthly schedule. By the time things really began to roll, Dave and I ditched *VV* and *N!S!T!* to concentrate on *MONSTER! INTERNATIONAL* as a full-

# ARE *MONSTERS* ESSENTIAL TO A FILM'S PLOT?

## --OR-- THIS ISLAND EARTH: THE *MUTANT* CONTROVERSY.

If the mutant didn't show up to threaten our heros in **THIS ISLAND EARTH**, then it wouldn't have harmed the plot one bit. But, without that nasty ol' BEM, then the film would have suffered in one big way: finacially! Universal felt they had to toss in this beastie for the audience and cash pull. Science fiction in the cinema has suffered a lot from this mental meshing that film production busses have put it through. Very few truely intelligent SF films have been sucessful without a *MONSTER* or two to threaten the crew or run off with the only female team member. And this attitue towards one of the most abused cinematic generes is both a sad and tired one. Having *MONSTERS* in a film can have its good points though. I'm sure that a hell of a lot of people wouldn't have gone to see **THIS ISLAND EARTH** if it didn't have that ugly mutant in it. It did add some excitement to the film and probably spurned a lot of kids who saw it in the theatres as well as on TV into drawing it and tring to physically replicate the creature for play or amature film ( I made mutant faces on paper bags to wear, and I once had a posable mutant I got for Christmas one year ). In that respect *MONSTERS* are an intricate part of any film, even though their very presence aren't needed. Maybe the fact that Universal actually believed in the film enough to make it in colour would support the idea of a creature that wasn't even hinted at in the original Raymond F. Jones novel from which the film was based.

THE GREATEST *DUELS* THE DEADLIEST

THE GREATEST *DUELS* THE DEADLIEST
*GODZILLA vs THE SMOG MONSTER*
COLOR ... DOLORSCOPE    An American International Release
©1972 American International Pictures, Inc.

*GODZILLA vs THE SMOG MONSTER*

# KOLCHAK THE NIGHT STALKER......

I loved this show when it first came out. What a cool idea: have this reporter that no one likes track down monsters, kill them, sometimes with some flimsy evidence, but no one believes his wild tales. There were times when the monsters were down right embarrassing ( the dinosaurman and the robot episodes come quickly to my mind ), and then there were those truly terrifying beasties: the dream induced boogieman, the Indian spirit monster, the Hindu demon, and the ultimate in Jack the Ripper. After **THE OUTER LIMITS**, **KOLCHAK** was the best of the monster anthologies. And why hasn't there been a good one ever since? Not even on cable or foreign TV? **DR. WHO** has had its share of original and sometimes frightful ( not never really convincing ) MONSTERS and aliens. The new **STAR TREK** lacks any interesting offerings ( and considering that there are thousands of inhabited planets talked about on the show you would at least imagine some interesting non-humanoid monsters to show up with more frequency ). There is even a new show called **MONSTERS** from the creators of **TALES FROM THE DARKSIDE** ( which lacked any neat monsters, with the exception of the creature created by Tom Savini in the episode: **IN THE CLOSET** ) which, so far, lacks in any downright terrifying monsters. The programme instead attempts a failed tongue-in-cheek appeal for all those smart-ass college kids out there. It's a pitiful show. **FREDDY'S NIGHTMARE** is equally dumb.... this mad-slasher-cum- bad-dream monger doesn't even pick on teenagers in this series. The creep just cracks stupid puns and one-liners then proceeds to ( for the most part ) dispatch adults. Give me enough cash and I'll produce a monster anthology that will scare the living pants off of anyone. It would be intelligent as well as frightening. Nasty as well as finely crafted. And there will be truly amazing and original stories and creepy-crawlies, shivers, and, well, MONSTERS!!!!! However, while I may have a whole drawer full of neat scripts and a head full of production sketches and directional thoughts, no one nowadays will even attempt to touch an intelligent, adult and crafty anthology . It just is too risky for today's television. **KOLCHACK** wasn't taken off because of it's rating. We all know that. It was pulled because Silverman didn't like horror...he would rather have brainless and sexist programmes like **THREE'S COMPANY** flood the airwave. Yuck. For those of you that yearn for the olden days of violent, and incredibly great, gut-wrenching television terror, then you...you who have cable...can tune into WGR Saturdays 8pm ( Eastern Time ) for two entire episodes, back to back, of **KOLCHACK**! Sit back and enjoy a rare treat. In these days of lame-brain anthologies. And for those of you who don't get WGR on your cable, check out your nearest super-video store 'cause the series is a comin' out on video!

---

## NEXT ISSUE ( Monday, December 19th ) : More *MONSTER!* films to come!

fledged magazine. *M!I* and *Highball* (our celebrated nudie movie mag) hit the big time with real distribution and slick offset printing. Many of you know what happened next. The 'zine/comic bubble burst in the late '90s. Dave and I ran out of money and we called it quits.

It's 2014, and both variants of *MONSTER!* are coming back. In your hands you hold the very first issue of the classic *MONSTER!*-style digest. This will be a monthly publication which I will co-edit with my buddy Steve Fenton, the mastermind behind the essential Canadian 'zines *Panicos* and *Killbaby*, and contributor to practically all the most important fanzines from the "Golden Age". Also welcome aboard Louis Paul, the editor/writer behind *The Blood Times*, who will be contributing a monthly column of monsterific reviews. As with the original digest,

*MONSTER!* will have a somewhat chaotic layout.

And, yes, I am still involved with *Weng's Chop*. Brian Harris and Tony Strauss and I love covering different genres and media formats in different magazines. That much will never change.

Oh, and if you're interested, I plan on a three-volume reprint series of books that will cover (almost) all of the issues of *MONSTER!* and *MONSTER! INTERNATIONAL*. *Almost* all the issues. I...um...cannibalized some images and articles from earlier issues to use in later ones. Tore them apart.

Like a zombie.

Like a MONSTER!

*- Tim Paxton*

# REVIEWS

First off, I have a very specific definition of "monster" when it comes to reviews. A monster movie is a film wherein the antagonist(s) is non-human in origin. That origin can be one found in a natural state or a transfigured one. For example: a scaly swamp creature of unknown origin (preferably prehistoric) or an alien beastie is natural, while a vampire, werewolf, ghost and zombie (dead or altered by science) are changed humans and thus transfigured monsters. Mad slashers are not. Crazy people who are cannibals are not. Politicians are not. I may waffle sometimes, but I usually stick to my guns on what constitutes MONSTER: a wonderful beast!

On a side-note: If you truly love the genre, may I suggest tracking down and purchasing the book A Monster is Loose – In Tokyo, by the late Vernon Grant. This is one of the books that transformed my early life. I bought it when I was ten with money I had saved up from my allowance. This small volume is crammed full of weird, sexy, and funny comics from an American serviceman stationed in Japan during the 1960s and '70s. This was where I first learned about the word, kaijū (怪獣). The first panel of the book (see above) is a classic. A rare and invaluable book if you can find it.

# SUBCONTINENTAL HORRORS
## Two Monstrous Movies from India

## HATYARIN ~ *"The Perilous Witch"*
1991, D: Vinod Talwar
*Starring: Birbal, Deepak Parashar, Javed Khan, Raza Murad, Sunil Dhawan , Amita Nangia,and Jamuna*

Monster movies are not all that common in Indian fantasy films. Sure, there are loads of demons and fearful ogres in the oodles of Hindu devotional films that were churned out in the past 100+ years of Subcontinental Cinema, but I'm not counting those appearances. Demons are central characters to most any devotional film. No, I'm talking about good old sectarian-based monsters. These things have appeared as hairy beasts, scaly creatures, or, in the case of the supernatural protagonist from **HATYARIN**, a rotten zombie witch. Their scarcity in Indian movies makes them oddities in a canon filled to the brim with ghosts and possessed humans.

The film opens with a traditional Hindu wedding in progress. A mysterious and beautiful wide-blue-eyed woman[1] (actress Jamuna in an unnamed role of The Woman in

---

1 We know right away that there's going to be supernatural trouble because the Woman in White flashes those baby blues. Blue eyes are very uncommon to the point of being unheard of unless you are possessed by a ghost, sprite, or demigod such as a Nag.

White, often referred to as The Widow) dressed all in white could be seen skulking around, glaring at the couple-to-be…that is, if anyone bothered to take note! At a crucial moment in the wedding vows she cuts the groom's coat-tails[2]. She then slips back, unnoticed, into the darkness outside of the party room.

Later as the party winds down, the bride retires upstairs to the honeymoon suite. But she is not alone. The mysterious woman is there, and she puts the whammy on the new bride. The young woman is led out of the house and placed in a waiting open carriage. Meanwhile, our excited groom enters the room ready for a night of pleasure. He spies what he believes is his bride lying in bed, and bends over to give her a smooch, but is horrified to find a grotesque monster in her place. The decaying horror springs out of the bed and bites him in the throat, ripping out a chunk of bloody meat (a sequence that appears to be cut short by some crude editing, possibly one of the many edits that had to be made for the film to pass the censor board of the time).

As the man dies, his bride is led by her kidnapper to a tree that lowers twitching vines from its branches and wraps them around the poor girl. She is then yanked up in the air, where she is stabbed with a large ceremonial knife. A gusher of blood splashes onto the

ground at the base of the tree, where it seeps into an open tomb. The woman laughs with glee and transforms into the bloated rotting visage of the monster. Cue title credits!

As the film progresses, more murders occur. In one instance a proud father attends his son's "High School Toy Show", where local children show off their favorite mechanical toys. His son's pride and joy is a dancing baby doll…but when it comes time for him to show his toy it refuses to function. The young boy is laughed at by his peers, and in frustration his father grabs the doll and dashes it to the ground. The toy then jumps up under its own power, emits a wail and loads of thick white smoke. The panicked audience stampedes and tramples the boy to death while out of the smoke the creature appears and bashes the father's head in against a wall.

The beast is unrelenting in its attacks on seemingly innocent people. Jamuna appears to another bride and groom on their honeymoon. The couple's car stalls on a dark roadway, and they are suddenly caught in a violent storm. The grotesque thing shows up and kills the husband, while his wife is carted off to be strung-up in the tree and stabbed; the red ichor draining into the mouth of a zombified *tantrik* who is in the tomb at the base of the hideous tree.

Why is the monster targeting the family members of three men, Kailash (Ajit Vachchani), Shambhu (Sudhir Pandey) and Vishambhar (Raza Murad), who have

---

2 This act signals something is afoot; I'm not sure what, but it has to be bad because we get that all-essential stock footage of a flash of lightning and crash of thunder that appears in many, *many* Indian films since the 1960s.

Sohal Production
PRESENTS
HATYARIN

RATAN BHATIA
DIMPLE ARTS

PRODUCED BY **DALWINDER SOHAL**
DIRECTED BY **VINOD TALWAR** MUSIC **NARESH SHARMA** LYRICS **SAMEER**

been life-long friends? What did they do to have their lives torn apart by the supernatural entity? Inspector Ravi (Deepak Parashar) must discover the truth, or Anita (Amita Nangia), his bride-to-be and the daughter of one of the men, could be the next target. Apparently there is a connection, but that won't be revealed until much later in the film.

Sensing that his time is nigh, Vishambhar, father of the next young couple targeted by the Woman in White, seeks help by contacting a powerful Shiva-based yogi (played by the terrific character actor Rajesh Vivek). However, a young police inspector suspects that the *tantrik* is somehow involved with the murder and has the holy man arrested and tossed in jail. Not the best move on the inspector's part, as the monster is still out there and attacks still another wedding party. This time the newlyweds are in the middle of consummating their marriage when disaster strikes. The young groom screams in pain as a huge gory monster hand erupts from his writing abdomen! He expires on the spot and his bride is grabbed by the throat and ends up on the killing tree. Her father races after the carriage only to finds his daughter's lifeless body hanging from the branches. Vishambhar is arrested for the crime, and committed to a hospital ward for observation. Unfortunately for him the monster tracks him down and drops a spinner ceiling fan on the poor guy.

Not knowing what else to do, Ravi releases the yogi, who agrees to help the officer solve this case. No matter the current state of affairs, Ravi is determined to marry Anita. On their wedding night he is almost strangled to death by an animated telephone cord, but he is rescued by the *tantrik* and his trusty sidekick, a floating "Happy Buddha" statue[3]. But they are too late to save Anita as she is whisked away in the car-

riage by the Woman in White. The *tantric* suspects the two women are en route to an old Kaali Maa temple, where the bodies of the previous murder victims were found. Anita is saved when the two men intercept Jamuna, and the demoness is herself tied to the tree. Once immobilized she gives tearful testimony as to why she has been killing everyone: Many years ago when Jamuna was a mortal, the three men whose family she has been terrorizing made a pact with an evil wizard named Kamlakh. The three had the wizard use his special powers to make Jamuna and her husband sign over their fortune to the greedy trio. Then the wizard gleefully killed the young pair. However, Jamuna's spirit returned and stabbed the wizard, who then cursed the ghost as he died. She must supply him with the blood of young virginal women from the families of the three men who had him kill Jamuna. So, this is why she has been on a bloody rampage.

This is where the movie gets wild. While the previous 120 minutes were full of very cool sequences, it's in the last seven minutes that Talwar lets his hair down. Clearly pissed that the wizard has possessed the soul of this tormented woman to do his bloodthirsty bidding, the yogi produces a magical flaming torch and tosses it into the open tomb. The wizard's body explodes into a fireball and all hell breaks loose as Jamuna is transformed into the corpse creature. What happens next can be best described as something akin to those wonderfully bizarre and frenetic Taiwanese fantasy and horror films from the 1980s. A violent storm blows up and the monster breaks free from its bonds to attack the trio. Folks are tossed all over the place as they attempt to kill the monster. The creature grows to giant proportions and swats at the humans, but is brought back down to size with a well-placed spell. Then the yogi brandishes various magical weapons (a spiked club, a large gold ball, a sword) to use against the thing. He manages to lop off first its arms and then its head. The grimacing noggin lands on the ground and immediately shoots forth a ribbon-like tongue to grab a hold of the young woman (see lobby card on page 6). The yogi saves her with a spell, but he is grabbed and tossed to the

---

3 Just for clarity, the statue is that of The Budai, which is a Chinese folkloric deity often confused with The Buddha, and has been often called, and is better known as, "The Laughing Buddha". He shows up in Taoist text and was eventually adopted in some Buddhist sects as a form of The Future Buddha.

ground by tentacles that emerge from the monster's bloody neck stump! The demon then grows another head and continues her assault on the young bride. Anita spies the old Kaali Maa statute and pleads to the ferocious black goddess to save her and her husband. The Goddess responds and gives one of her weapons to Ravi (this particular statue has a sword, trident, and other holy symbols), and he uses the blade to finally put an end to the horror. Cue happy dance number and…"The End"!

The overall walk-away experience of **HATYARIN** is one of satisfaction. If you have seen as many Indian horror films as I have, it is abundantly clear that Talwar was out to create a monster movie comparable with no other. Other subcontinental filmmakers were interested in the genre, but only a few could break away from tired conventions. The Malayalam director Baby produced what could be called the best South Asian variety of monster films during the 1980s and '90s, while Talwar worked primarily out of Bollywood. I guess you could toss in the Ramsays' films for comparison, but I always found most of them to be somewhat dull[4]. Their films had wonderfully-designed monsters that, with a few exceptions, rarely had much to do with the plots. Talwar took the traditional Woman in White witch/ghost motif (made popular by Baby's 1981 film **LIZA**) and incorporated the ghoulish horror of a reanimated corpse (something

[4] I've considered to give them another go though, and *MONSTER!* shall begin to run reviews of each of their monster movies starting in the next issue.

that Kanti Shah would later try in some of his productions). *And* he had the monster appear throughout the film in full glorious view of the camera. No creeping about in the shadows for this beastie, you get to see its ugly mug *all the time*.

Actress Jamuna, who plays the gorgeous Woman in White, appeared in a few other thrillers, but never seemed to get anywhere in Bollywood. Some of her other films include Ajit Asthana's 1994 spook flick **ANDHERA**, and **KAFAN** (1990, D: Suri). She is often confused with the more famous Telugu actress Jamuna. Rajesh Vivek stars as the lanky, beetle-browed Good Yogi, a role he seems to be forever stuck playing since 1988 when he appeared as "Baba" (another word for yogi or master) in the Ramsay horror film **VEERANA**.

Despite all of its frightfully good bits, some great musical numbers and wonderful actors, **HATYARIN** was not a huge hit. This was to be Talwar's final directorial effort, exiting that position in the industry in order to produce action films. In a recent conversation with the director I learned that he is interested in returning to the horror genre. Apparently it was his first love, and with the resurgence of the genre in Indian cinema there may well be a chance that he might direct another monster movie; maybe a remake of this classic with a tad bit of modernization, but keep the effects "practical" and keep away from all the CG that plagues most Indian horror films.

That would be sweet.

# CHAMUNDA

1999, D: Kishan Shah

*Starring: Satnam Koul, Raaj Premi, Haider, Jyoti Rana, Arun Mathius, Shabnam, Razak Khan, Vinid Tripathi, and Anil Nagarath*

Whereas Talwar's **HATYARIN** is a fine example of a superior horror film that successfully integrates classic elements of Indian traditional supernatural entities with Western frights, **CHAMUNDA** misfires on all cylinders. The problem is not that the film lacks a substantial budget to deliver believable monster effects (sometimes that can be a blessing in disguise), but that somewhere between the first fifteen minutes and the last, the plot fragments into something dull and unimaginative.

The film opens in what looks like Mughal Empire-era India (making it around 1600 AD). A huge bald madman is running wild attacking and murdering people throughout the region. The creature is Samri, a black peacoat-wearing wizard (yes, 20th Century English nautical wear in 17th Century India!) who drinks the blood of those he kills so as to magically render himself immortal. Samri mistakenly kills the daughter of the local regency, Raja Pratap Singh, and is hunted down and captured. Faced with execution, Samri curses the Raj that he will someday return from the dead and take his revenge. With that utterance, he is dispatched. Samri's head is chopped off and placed in a special box sealed with a small *trishul*, the three-pronged trident of the Hindu deity Lord Shiva. The giant's other half is placed in a separate casket and wrapped in chains, and both are kept within the Raj's estate so he can keep an eye on the body parts.

VCD sleeve art.

Samri the monstrous wizard is cornered by someone sticking the holy *trishul* of Shiva in his face.

We fast-forward 300-odd years to 1999, and the descendants of Pratap Singh have decided to move back into their ancestral home, the mansion that houses the remains of the wizard. Uh-oh, this could spell trouble! Umm, no. For the next hour we are bored to tears with sad musical numbers (by budget soundtrack composer Sawan Kumar Sawan), manic pontification by the film's heavy (played by the always-grotesque Anil Nagrath), and inane comedic moments brought to you by actors better off not named.

Suddenly, as if under orders by a hideous strength, the mansion's disfigured handyman removes the holy *trishul* from atop the box and steals the head of the wizard. He runs to the sealed chest, kicks off the chains, and lowers Samri's noggin onto his body. With a flash of (stock footage) lightning, the monster is whole again. He thanks his servant with a hearty (and fatal) choking, then promptly rises from his box and begins another reign of terror. The good folks of the nearby hamlet will have none of the murder and mayhem, and prepare for some good ol' monster-hunting (torches and clubs in-hand). This scene in particular I found fascinating. Here we are in 1999 and "villagers" are *still* out to get the monster equipped with clubs, scythes, and torches. Oh, and one of the guys is wearing a damn fine Tin Tin T-shirt!

After annihilating a few of the less-fortunate villagers, Samri then concentrates his killing spree on the descendants of Raj Pratap Singh. He kills one of the girls, and sets his sights on still another. Samri corners her in the mansion and proceeds to choke her. The boyfriend comes to her rescue but he is knocked aside. Bloodied but unbowed by his close encounter with the monster, he happens to see the discarded *trishul* on a nearby tabletop (how convenient!). After a long, rambling proclamation about good and evil and how he's going to stop Samri, etc. (at this point you're thinking, okay, so by the time he's done with his oratory the monster would have finished with the girl anyway), he jabs the giant with weapon. Samri stumbles about and then immediately falls to the floor and expires.

Now that that's over with, the survivors gather around a statue of Shiva. There they put the trident in the statue's hand and pray and praise the god (which is not that unusual of an ending for an Indian horror film). The End.

If you are a connoisseur of Indian horror films like I am, this lackluster production shouldn't give you too much of a sore butt. And knowing that Krishan Shah is the brother of Kanti Shah (India's notorious indie sleaze-meister of the 1990s-2000s) then the slackness of **CHAMUNDA** shouldn't come as much of a surprise. No doubt working on a minuscule budget, Shah scraps the idea of raiding the nearby costume shop for a rubber fright mask and

Just when it looks like it's the end of another of the Raj's descendants, Samri is run through by a *trishul*.

instead chooses to slather the actor playing Samri in greasepaint instead. The end result is actually rather refreshing, as it gives the Wizard a certain air of dignity. Better crudely-applied theatrical makeup than a floppy Don Post knockoff.

For more films by Krishan and Kanti Shah, check out *Weng's Chop* #5 and my article on the low-budget thrillride that *was* the Indian Indie film scene.

All praise Shiva! The End.

# MORE MONSTERS NEXT ISSUE!

There have been very few Bollywood monster movies released in the United States. Of the ones that have, most all of them have been by one family of filmmakers. Come to think of it, the DVDs that did come out with four of the most popular of the Ramsay creature features are now woefully out of print. Never fear, because starting with *MONSTER!* #2 we will be serving up all of their monster movies in (I hope) lengthy reviews. I may not have enjoyed them as much as I did the films by Vinod Talwar, but almost all of the movies have cool supernatural entities of one form or another in them.

The image to the left represents how I usually buy my Indian movies. This is a DVD collection of three of the more obscure Ramsay monster films. Most of these compilations come in this horrid 3-in-1 DVD format and the video quality is very poor due to the high compression. They also lack any form of bonus material (yep, no English subtitles). Films are also available as single movies on VCDs (which have the same resolution as a VHS tape recorded in SLP mode). To make matters worse, the video masters for these DVDs or VCDs are almost always sourced from crummy VHS tapes from the 1980s or '90s (complete with tape damage and drop-out). What I put

Back in the decade of the classic MONSTER! fanzine, a type of themed article such as this would have been written in one sitting after a night of binging on the chosen subject matter. Line 'em up and knock 'em down. That was in the days before Internet access was as easily available…fast or cheap. There was no Google, YouTube or Netflix back then, and file-sharing (via bit-torrent) has come a long way since The Community used to swap digital files via floppy or ZiP disk. Nowadays it's much easier to approach an article in bit and pieces, saving information into The Cloud and so forth.

The beauty of MONSTER! is the spontaneity that comes from collecting reviews for any particular issue. Take for instance how this article came into existence: While on a particularly odd line of research for Weng's Chop, I came across the poster art for the film *DEVIL'S EXPRESS* (1976). Scouring YouTube for a full version of the film, I was led to the alternate title for the Taiwanese black magic film *THE DEVIL* (which is on YouTube as "The.Devil's.Express"). That bit of investigation uncovered the Thai film *TRAIN OF THE DEAD* (2007), which in turn drew the interest of Takeshi Furusawa's *GHOST TRAIN* (Otoshimono, 2006). Then the poster art for *DEVIL'S EXPRESS* struck me as somewhat similar to the monster locomotive period piece *HORROR EXPRESS* (1972). Funny how that played out!

# TICKET TO TERROR

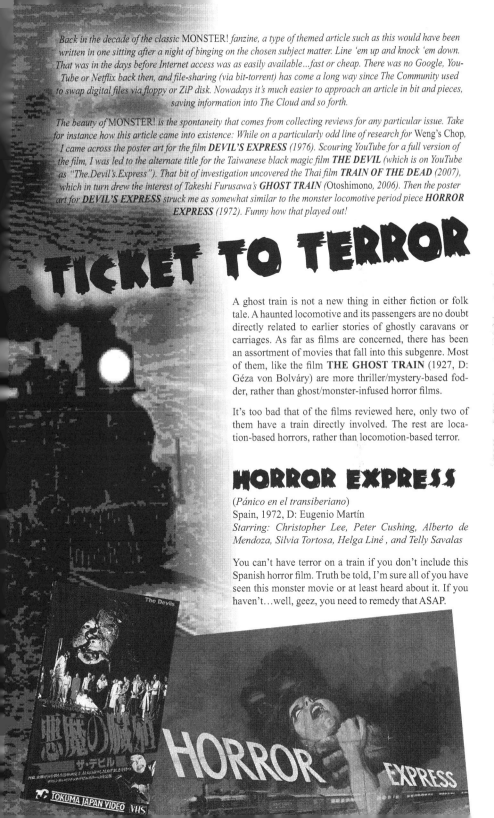

A ghost train is not a new thing in either fiction or folk tale. A haunted locomotive and its passengers are no doubt directly related to earlier stories of ghostly caravans or carriages. As far as films are concerned, there has been an assortment of movies that fall into this subgenre. Most of them, like the film **THE GHOST TRAIN** (1927, D: Géza von Bolváry) are more thriller/mystery-based fodder, rather than ghost/monster-infused horror films.

It's too bad that of the films reviewed here, only two of them have a train directly involved. The rest are location-based horrors, rather than locomotion-based terror.

## HORROR EXPRESS

(*Pánico en el transiberiano*)
Spain, 1972, D: Eugenio Martín
*Starring: Christopher Lee, Peter Cushing, Alberto de Mendoza, Silvia Tortosa, Helga Liné , and Telly Savalas*

You can't have terror on a train if you don't include this Spanish horror film. Truth be told, I'm sure all of you have seen this monster movie or at least heard about it. If you haven't…well, geez, you need to remedy that ASAP.

El Expresso del Diablo

50,000 años de muerte acechan en el METRO

con
WARHAWK TANZANIA
Larry Fleischman
y Sam De Fazio
Panavision Technicolor

PRESENTADO POR IMASU J. SADA     DISTRIBUIDA POR     TELEFILMS INTERNACIONAL, S. A.

The film opens: it's early into the new century when scientific exploration and thirst for knowledge knows no bounds. The corpse of a monstrous ape-thing has been uncovered in China by a team of European scientists led by Christopher Lee. The creature is packed away in ice and the crate loaded onto the Trans-Siberian Express for its trip to Moscow. Aboard the train is a rival scientist played by Peter Cushing. Cushing plans on sneaking a peek at what's in the crate, no matter what the cost. Of course, that leads to trouble…

Thanks to scientific curiosity and a sizeable bribe to the right person, the creature, rightfully assumed to be dead, is defrosted and starts killing off passengers on the train. The monster gobbles the minds of its prey, leaving their bodies with white-boiled eyes and faces streaked with blood, and is able to absorb the explicit and implicit memory of its victims, also body-hopping in the process. The essence of the creature passes from one human to the next as it gathers information about our world. You see, the thing is an alien that has been transferring its cognitive attribute from one terrestrial form to another since the days of the dinosaurs. The creature plans on amassing all the current scientific knowledge of 1902 so that it can rebuild its spaceship and leave our little rock…possibly to return with an invading army of still more mind-gobbling monsters.

That's the gist of the plot. What makes this film a wonderful chapter in monsterdom is the terrific pacing and the fact that its director, the talent-

ed Eugenio Martín, has crafted a science fiction film disguised as a 20th Century costume drama. I missed seeing this film in the theatre in 1972, but did manage to catch **GODZILLA VS. THE SMOG MONSTER** which, at the time, I thought was the pinnacle of everything that was cool about monsters (well, except when 'Zilla used his atomic breath to fly—that was a moment of sheer embarrassment for me as my friends turned to me in the theatre and laughed). I had to wait until the late '70s when **HORROR EXPRESS** played local Cleveland TV. And when I did finally see the film my mind was blown. **HORROR EXPRESS** struck me as a distant cousin to a *Quatermass* film. An earth scientist is up against an alien terror that is dead-set in taking over the Earth. For those of you who need some schooling, do yourself a favor and stream or buy the best 1950s SF monster films ever: **THE QUATERMASS XPERIMENT** (1955, D: Val Guest), **QUATERMASS 2** (1957, D: Val Guest), and the 1967 must-see **QUATERMASS AND THE PIT** (D: Roy Ward Baker). Just Google those titles. 'Nuff said.

## DEVIL'S EXPRESS

USA, 1976, D: Barry Rosen
*Starring: Warhawk Tanzania, Thomas D. Anglin, Fred Berner, Stefan Czapsky, Sam Defazio, Thomas Doran, and Jane Landis*

The original title for **DEVIL'S EXPRESS** was **GANG WARS**, and the poster for that initial re-

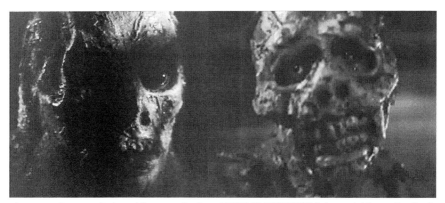

I swear, who ever designed the monster from **DEVIL'S EXPRESS** (*above right*) must've had **HORROR EXPRESS** (above left) in his sites. Structurally, the headpiece looks like they took a Don Post skull mask (commercially available since 1968) and applied wax and latex to it. Check out image (below) from **HALLOWEEN 3: SEASON OF THE WITCH** (1982, D: Tommy Lee Wallace ) and you'll see what I mean.

lease was none-too-exciting. I'm sure the film did better with the newly revised title and artwork. At least if you couldn't pull in the gang crowd, you can almost always count on the horror film fans. Given that the plot involved kung fu, gangs in NYC, and a monster prowling the subways, then the title change and more supernaturally exploitative poster art was in order (it definitely caught my eye). Now that I have re-watched **HORROR EXPRESS**, it seems to me that Spanish film must've been on the mind of writer/director Barry Rosen. Even the monsters are somewhat similar.

As the film opens we are told that it is China 200AD, and a large wooden coffin is being lowered into an underground cavern. A saffron-robed monk utters something mystical as a large, jewel-encrusted pendant is place on the box, and then all those who are witness to the ritual are killed by a sword-wielding monk. The remaining warrior-monk guts himself. Something really horrid must have been in that box for them to take all those hardcore precautions.

Fast-forward a few hundred years to modern day New York City—somewhere in Harlem or another of the many depressed neighborhoods. We are introduced to Luke (Warhawk Tanzania), the tall and lean master of martial arts and star of the film. He is a black man of action, full of piss and vinegar, spiteful of The Man. He spouts equal measures of Zenny bullshit and street-talking bad-assery. Luke decides that he has learned all he can learn from the masters in New York City, and takes a trip abroad to expand and disciple with a renowned master in Hong Kong. For some odd reason he brings his buddy Rodan (Wilfredo Roldan) along with him.

Rodan is a distrustful (of The Man), thieving piece of trash, so why not? Maybe he'll learn something. Broaden his horizons, etc.

Nope, the little shit goes off on his own once they get to Hong Kong, and gets into trouble. Rodan manages to find the box hidden in the underground cavern, and pockets the jewel. Come sundown when Luke and Rodan board their boat back to the States, a gooey monster breaks out of the box and stumbles out of the cave. The creature makes its way to the boat and attacks a man, taking possession of his body (somehow) in the process and stowing away onboard for the return trip to America. Once the ship reaches the docks of New York, the monster-possessed man stumbles from the bowels of the boat. Because it fears sunlight (something we learn later on), the creatures makes its way to the subway system below the city. Once underground the monster bursts from the body of

Luke confronts the terror of the subway.

the unfortunate human. This would have been a fairly cool sequence but, as with a lot of the cinematography in this film, if someone had bothered to turn a light on while it was being filmed, then maybe we could have made out just what was going on.

Meanwhile, as the creature establishes itself in the subway and Luke resumes his studies at a local bar, Rodan and one of his buddies meet with a Chinese drug dealer. They stiff their supplier and make off with a bag of cocaine. The gang in charge of the illicit trafficking in that part of NYC isn't too happy with Rodan and his buddy, and an all-out gang war ensues. The black gang is led by Rodan (and somehow associated with Luke), who really hates the Chinese. The overlong battle sequences that follow are full of mind-blowingly bad martial arts. We see all sorts of weird kung-fu posturing and prancing, wild kicks and punches (that are nowhere near their targets), swords as well as iron pipes, and even wooden beams are utilized. In no way are any of the fights in this film realistic, but they sure are fun to watch!

The police are baffled by the bloody bodies that turn up in the subways and attribute them to the gang wars that are in full swing. Even a crazy priest is called in for no apparent reason other than to scream about "God is dead, Muhammad is dead, Buddha is dead" to a gaggle of confused onlookers. Lucky for us he's played by the late actor/comedian Brother Theodore, making **DEVIL'S EXPRESS** one of the few films he had an acting role in during his wonderful career. (Brother who, you ask? Google him!) Incidentally, some demented if all-too-brief introductory narration by Brother Theodore can be heard in Al Adamson's patchwork US/Filipino sci-fi schlocker **HORROR OF THE BLOOD MONSTERS** (1970).

During one of the gang scuffles in the present film, Rodan has the jewel he lifted off the box stolen by one of his Chinese opponents. He is then chased

into the subway, where he runs into the monster. There he is killed when the creature smashes the man's face into an electrical box. When Luke learns of his obnoxious buddy's demise he is determined to discover what is behind all the murders. Luke makes peace with the Chinese gang and is taken to their spiritual leader, a disfigured old man. The master knows the ancient mystical art of demonology, and informs the kung fu master that he is up against a Chinese demon. Only by returning the demon to the jewel can Luke stop all the killing. Luke is given the jewel and specific instructions on how to link his mind with that of the Chinese elder; in doing so they can combine their spiritual forces and put an end to the demon once and for all.

Our hero descends into the subway and is confronted by various psychic forces which he must defeat: a fierce female fighter and a set of karate-dealing twins. Luke dispatches them with ease using his superior training only to come face-to-face with the huge ugly demon. After an assortment of frenzied fist and foot volleys, Luke manages to strike the creature to the ground where he grabs it around the neck and forces its essence into the jewel. The End.

As exciting as all this sounds, the kung fu action is pitiful and the dialogue...well, it's from the "Look here, *honky*, a brother can take care of himself. He needs *no* help from *The Man*" school of scripting. Subtle this film is not! Roldan here reprises (?) his role of Rodan, which he "mastered" (with Tanzania) in the previous urban chop-socky epic

**BLACK FORCE** (a.k.a. **FORCE + FOUR**, 1975, D: Michael Fink). And lucky for us, his obnoxious character was killed in **DEVIL'S EXPRESS,** or Rodan could very well have ended up in another sorry film.

Now, the monster itself is fairly cool, although throughout its brief appearances in the film it is obscured in darkness. The creature resembles a rotting corpse, and stands taller than Tanzania, who must be at least 6' 5" (if you count his power afro!). It's a pity that the monster wasn't treated with a little more respect. As for a better-looking Chinese monster that resembles an oozing corpse, may I suggest 魔胎 / *Mo tai* / **DEVIL'S FETUS** (1983, D: Hung-Chuen Lau). Now *that's* a monster movie that is worth tracking down for a night of grotesque creature action; especially one that doesn't feature extended scenes of extremely fake "kung fu".

I was hard-pressed to find an actual sample of the Asian variety of train-related terror. As with their Euro cousins there is more to be found at a haunted tunnel or monster-riddled train station rather than aboard a locomotive. A good example of a supernatural train station is in a wonderful segment at the beginning of the Korean film 구미호 / *Gumiho* / **THE FOX WITH NINE TAILS** (1994, D: Park Heon-soo). In this scene we see a variety of souls on their way to hell being manhandled by unsavory demons. Although the film is played more for laughs, it is one of my favorite films of the fox-demon-spirit sub-genre.[1]

The Japanese-made post-**RINGU** (リング, 1998, D: Hideo Nakata ) 2006 film オトシモノ / *Otoshimono* / **THE GHOST TRAIN** (D: Takeshi Furusawa) doesn't carry the fantastic weight of Sukhum Mathawanit's train-ride to Hell, ชุมทางรถไฟผี/*Chum Thaang Rot Fai Phii* / **TRAIN OF THE DEAD** (2007), but it does manage to pack a creepy wallop with its entire haunted train tunnel full of ghoulish dead people. That is, if you can make it through the first 90 minutes of the film's drab and sulking plot.

*And speaking of Sukhum Mathawanit...*

# TRAIN OF THE DEAD

(ชุมทางรถไฟผี / *Chum Thaang Rot Fai Phii*)
Thailand, 2007, D: Sukhum Mathawanit
*Starring: Kett Thantup, Savika Chaiyadej, Sura Theerakon, and Chaleumpol Tikumpornteerawong*

---

1 A shout out to Jeff Kwitny's 1989 Italian produced horror film **AMOK TRAIN**, which features devil worshipers stalking a Romanian locomotive looking for a young American virgins to sacrifice to "an ancient evil". No monster appears per se, although there is a hint of one by the film's conclusion.

**THE GHOST TRAIN**

---

**TRAIN OF THE DEAD** is a Thai horror ghost film which, true to its name, delivers on the spookiness of a haunted train. Not a horrible film, but as with a lot of Thai productions I've seen over the years, everything seems rushed. At least the amount of asinine humor has been reduced to a few annoying scenes, though.

The film opens as a group of men are sleeping in an abandoned warehouse. One of the men, Muerd, awakes to see a ghost and has a terrifying encounter with it. But it was all a dream...or was it? Later he and his buddies rob a kindergarten (yes, a kindergarten!) and make off with a handful of cash. While fleeing the police they kidnap Toh, a young man who witnesses their crimewave. Instead of killing him, the

Sexy Thai ghosts never bother me in the least.

The gang is made to pay for their past transgression at the spectral hands of those they killed.

gang takes Toh along for the ride as they stow-away on a train headed out of Bangkok. The train is full of rich folk, and the gang sees a chance of increasing their day's booty by shaking the passengers down. But this is no ordinary train, as Muerd soon realizes, for he sees the passengers as what they truly are: ghosts. Toh meets a mysterious young woman on the train named Ratree, who begs him "not to commit any more sin". For you see, this is a train that is taking the dead to their final judgment, and Toh is not scheduled to be delivered to Hell's gate just yet...

While the final half of the film meanders a bit, the pace picks up when the spooks begin to make them-

El creador de "THE EYE" en una nueva fantasía de terror.

BANGKOK HAUNTED

La muerte no es el fin.

selves known to the gang. I didn't find it all that horrible of an experience. The film does suffer from the cheapness of the production, which includes a rinky-dink synth soundtrack and some really sub-par computer graphics (although all of the gore sequences are practical effects). What visuals there are present are executed well, and their weird cartoonish application to the sequences in the film does add to the overall supernatural unease. But the animated train used for the film...man, you guys could have sprung for some stock footage, or something!

One of the more entertaining aspects of the film is the variety of actors. All of the women are young and pretty (well, except for the old ghost that haunts the train), and the male gang members are your typical stereotypes, if you are familiar with Thai film. I did enjoy the crazy boss of the gang, who chews up almost every scene he's in with what must be his tribute to an agitated Toshirô Mifune.

I've sat through worse films on the SyFy Channel or those I found streaming on NetFlix.

Looking for superior Thai frights? Check out the 2001 film ผีสามบาท / **BANGKOK HAUNTED** by Oxide Pang Chun and Pisut Praesangeam

*A Way Overlong & Very Self-Indulgent Dissertation on a Mexploitation Masterpiece:*

# BLUE DEMON CONTRA CEREBROS INFERNALES

## ("Blue Demon vs. the Infernal Brains")

### Reviewed by Steve Fenton

Mexico, 1966, D: Chano Urueta

Now pay attention, *niños*, because this is a lengthy appraisal of a film that is well worth every last word of the lovingly verbose attention I shall be lavishing upon it.

Firstly, to avoid any potential confusion amongst all you Mexploitation novices out there (wherever ye may be, ya newbs!), other than by their obvious rudimentary thematic similarities **BLUE DEMON CONTRA LOS CEREBROS INFERNALES** has nothing whatsoever to do with either **SANTO EN CEREBRO DEL MAL** ("*Santo in the Evil Brain*", 1958) or **SANTO CONTRA EL CEREBRO DIABÓLICO** ("*Santo vs. the Diabolical Brain*", 1961), okay?

For the present film, great pop-out Pop Art opening titles showing assorted hand-cut, human-shaped silhouettes caught in static action poses are glued atop solid-coloured backgrounds, all overlaid by the jauntily catchy jazz-rock theme which is replayed

repeatedly throughout the running time without ever grating on your nerves (kudos must go out to Mexcinema maestro Gustavo César Carrión for the ear-pleasing ditty). This music—driving electric rhythm guitar laden with percolating percussion and blaring brass doing their best to keep up—sounds great as star BD, complete with his cool, flowing, sparkle-speckled azure cape, smacks would-be *secuestradores* ("kidnappers") around next to—of all things—a large red pagoda (evidently situated somewhere in the vicinity of Mexico City's Chinatown?).

Our star definitely possessed one of the Mexi-flexi world's more memorable and coolest trademarked costumes: eye-catching, functional, fetishistic and snazzy in equal degree; complete with silver-trimmed blue mask and tights, and his funky shoulder-covering-but-torso-baring-full-length cloak (which he generally doffed during off-screen tussles but often kept on for his onscreen ones, so long as things didn't get too down 'n' dirty. After all, custom-tailored capes cost *mucho dinero*, don't you know). Presumably because of the commercial successes of Blue Demon's then-recent screen debut (**BLUE DEMON, EL DEMONIO AZUL** [1964]), the wrestler was now largely known just as "Blue Demon" in English, even within Spanish versions of his films. He was often referred to merely as the even-less-formal "Blue". In **CEREBROS INFERNALES**, Blue is given a slight supernatural tinge by his remarkable ability to disappear (i.e., blink out like a light) then rematerialize seconds later in a different spot within the same general vicinity. He also displays this uncanny knack in other films such as **EL MUNDO DE LOS MUERTOS** ("*The World of the Dead*", 1969), but here it is depicted with dynamically tacky panache via having our hero move around in front of a static camera to pose in different spots, then merely have the editor chop out all the chunks of transitional frames in-between so that Blue "appears" to have hopped from spot to spot in the blink of an eye without you even noticing him go from A to B. That said, for all I know they might even have accomplished it all in-camera and eliminated the middle man (i.e., the editor) completely. However crude, this "space-hopping" technique

I5

DP daubed on his kids' paint-box colour scheme ("*en colores*" and then some!) at times make the film appear to have been shot in a full three dimensions—possibly even *four*—rather than merely "flat" (BD in 3D: *WOW!*).

While uttering such tongue-twisting hi-tech humdingers as "*encephalos electrolicos*", criminal mastermind Dr. Sántez (frequent Mex heavy Noe Murayama, an actor of Hispano-Japanese heritage who also popped-up in a couple Spaghetti Westerns, including Sergio Sollima's **CORRI, UOMO, CORRI** [a.k.a. **RUN, MAN, RUN**, 1967, Italy/France]) runs a scientific complex peopled by robotized men and female droids à la Vincent Price's comely creations in Bava's **DR. GOLDFOOT AND THE GIRL BOMBS** (*Le spie vengono dal semifreddo*, 1966). There's also a quasi-hunchback gimping sinisterly about, played with a bit of a stoop and a shuffling limp by co-writer Fernando Osés, a Spanish (i.e., born in Spain) wrestler/actor who frequently wrote parts for himself into his scenarios, and frequently mixed it up with El Santo onscreen for some memorably energetic, set-trashing rough 'n' tumble, often reminiscent of those spirited stunt smash'emups seen in old Republic serials (involving the likes of fall guy Dale Van Sickel). In an amusing scene here worthy of cult cinematic sub-genius Ted V. "**ASTRO ZOMBIES**" Mikels, generic "Igor" Osés—

nonetheless instills some funky kinesis into what might otherwise have merely remained a strip of lifeless two-dimensional celluloid. Energetic infusions such as Blue's "spot-shifting" combined with the delusory, gawp-inducing palette from which the

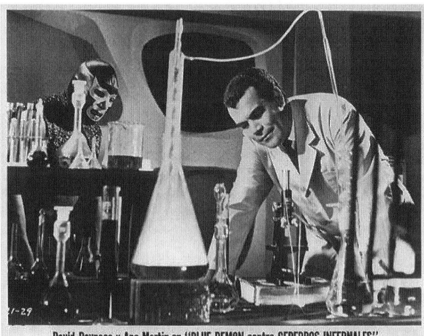

**David Reynoso y Ana Martin en "BLUE DEMON contra CEREBROS INFERNALES"**
con BLUE DEMON, VICTOR JUNCO, NOE MURAYAMA y DAGOBERTO RODRIGUEZ • A COLORES • A1382

clad in a sky-blue surgical smock as an apparent failed experimental (lobotomy?) subject of his master's—shuffles out carrying a big bowl full of fresh brains as if serving hors d'oeuvres at a dinner party.

While in '66 the so-called Psychedelic Era wasn't quite yet in full swing north-of-the-border, you'd never know it to see this movie. After all, Mexicans were messing about with psychedelic drugs for centuries before LSD and hippies ever came along; just witness all that mescaline (it ain't called "Mescal" tequila for nothing!) and peyote buttons ("magic mushrooms") the natives had been consuming since who knows when. So they had a firm handle on psychedelia long before the *gringo* counterculture ever got their mitts on it. On top of its riotous color scheme, elsewhere, the mad medico's lab seen herein is a Day-Glo wet dream/nightmare smothered in all sorts of utterly meaningless coloured lights—including an old TV set whose screen has been refitted with blinking multi-hued Xmas tree bulbs!—while various zapping gadgets give off arcs of live electricity, all accompanied by assorted electronic blips, bleeps and beeps on the audio track. Futurism has seldom looked so tackily tawdry as this!

In the mandatory *lucha libre* material, legendary non-masked wrestling wildman Rodolfo *Cavernario* ("Caveman") Galindo battles BD, who is referred to bilingually as both *El Demonio Azul* and Blue Demon by the speed-talking commentator. Not only does he battering-ram his opponent's head into a turnbuckle, but Galindo at one point also seeks to bite Blue's *foot* off (!?), although our titular rassler soon ties his savage opponent into a limb pretzel. Meanwhile, intercut with the ring action, a mad doctor triumvirate headed up by Dr. Sántez works on the skull of a patient strapped to their operating table. A close-up pile of pulsing red glop indicates that his brain has just been removed. The "makeup effects" here are revealed to be lamentably crude, with over-ripe animal offal posing as "transplanted human brain matter" to highly convincing effect (not!).

Although BD later re-enters the ring to tangle with middle-aged, barefoot, but no less ornery—and even uglier—*rudo* Jesús Velásquez (ring-name "*El Murciélago*" ["The Bat"]), cheesecake is next on the menu, with a perkily vivacious and pleasantly buxom Mexican Indian go-go gal doing the shimmy-shake in a tasseled bikini, much to guest star Víctor Junco's quiet approval. He merely raises his eyebrows with suave sophistication and puffs on his smoke while watching (here the camera's eye becomes both his and ours, zeroing-in on the cheerfully smiling dancer's switching hips and twitching butt). After this, we spend time at a beat scene discotheque where frantically frugging teenyboppers in miniskirts and go-go boots—and let's not forget tight sweaters stretched smoothly over bullet-brassiered busts—groove to the happenin' jazz/rock 'n' roll onslaught of those brassy, horny saxmaniacs *El Klan* (a locally popular act, these boys appeared in more than one other film, as well as recording sundry vinyl). In another shot that looks like it jumped right out of a 3-D movie and into your lap, a Klan

Deadlier Than The Male: boffo bouffant robobabes appear at ringside to zap BD with their rayguns right in mid-bout.

horn-player blows cigarette fumes out through the bell of his instrument directly into the audience's faces—watch out for that second-hand smoke! As with much of the rest of the film, fast—if admittedly choppy—cutting combined with lively tuneage contribute greatly to this sequence's irrepressibly exuberant energy. Indeed, everybody seems to be having such a blast that it makes you wish you were there right along with them.

Following this welcome musical interlude, a carload of mammarian robot girls use their hi-tech K.O. gas pistols to abduct another prominent egghead for Dr. Sántez to yank the brainy brainpan out of. Missing brains with missing brains (or others on the hit-list) include Drs. Robles, Calvin and Jiménez. Such of his esteemed medical colleagues as have already been given the instant total brain-drain treatment now have their valuable, data-crammed cerebral matter on throbbing display beneath bell jars, with each involuntary donor's clearly identified by an attached hand-printed adhesive label bearing his name (don't you just love such anal-retentively organized compartmentalization!?). Head villain Murayama puts on endless practical demonstrations of his innovative surgical methods for assembled co-workers in the field, including Junco as one Dr. Karras [sic?], who, when not ogling starlets with suggestive intent merely stands around observing his host Murayama's activities while interjecting patronizingly supportive adjectives like "¡Stupendo, stupendo!" or "Muy bien" on a regular basis.

The Secreto Servicio, as represented by co-star David Reynoso (of whom, more later), are stumped by all this grey matter which has been going missing with alarming regularity; and by the silver-spray-painted skeleton—intended to represent a fleshless chromed cyborg armature!—that shows up in a cooler-locker drawer down at the local morgue (the end-result of a decomposed "dead" mandroid).

Under a stick-on beard, Reynoso poses as Dr. Vicente Morales, an alleged world-renowned boffin, so as to attract wanted attention from the brain-napping ring so that he may fall into their clutches and thus turn the tables on them. To this end, he is gassed out cold by the catty Katia and carted off by her buxotic robotic kittens. Now seems about the right time to mention the second-billed Reynoso's pre-disguised, barefaced appearance, who looks uncomfortably like—wait for it…future disgraced U.S. Prez Richard "Tricky Dickie" Nixon! I kid you not: from certain angles while making certain expressions, the likeness between the actor and the shady politico is most uncanny. Although the film was made years before both Nixon's presidency and the Watergate

scandal that brought about his fall from grace, there is even some stuff in here involving bugging devices used to eavesdrop on those whom Reynoso's character—who is respectfully addressed as Jefe ("Chief") by his female sidekick—deems necessary to be placed under covert surveillance. Said sidekick (played by girlishly cute, doll-like "redhead" Ana Martín) also functions as her boss' high-maintenance romantic interest of sorts.

What looks suspiciously like an electric soldering iron doubles as a "hi-tech" neurosurgery gizmo used for "trepanning" skulls. The trio of brains, pulsing under their respective bell jars, converse telepathically with Murayama, their thoughts heard amplified over loudspeakers. A similar "brain-pool" can also be seen in Federico Curiel's 1959-60 Neutrón trilogy (mostly in Part 3, LOS AUTOMATAS DE LA MUERTE ["The Death Robots", a.k.a. NEUTRON AGAINST THE DEATH ROBOTS]). As the doc converses with his bottled brains, BD bursts into the lab. Dr. Sántez mixes unstable chemicals together to cause a suicidal laboratory explosion that also consumes the bodiless brains. FIN.

In one of many stand-out scenes, that same frenetic theme music kicks in again when BD slugs, flips and generally manhandles a couple of robo-men (who save the special makeup department a bundle by simply looking like regular men with nary a hint of robot about them) alongside a big blue rocket ship mock-up standing next to a much taller oil derrick-like structure which also vaguely evokes a NASA launch-gantry (actually some sort of water tower?). While the tower looks authentic enough, the nearby rocket seems to have been some sort of standing set/prop—a local tourist attraction, perhaps? The rocket looks very solidly built and is a good 30 feet in height, so it seems unlikely that it could have been specially engineered for such a low-budget movie as this (it only appears in this single scene).

For BLUE DEMON CONTRA CEREBROS INFERNALES' single most exciting action stunt, a robo-man seeks to escape a further beating from Blue by scaling the ladder of that aforementioned metal pylon—which is at least 100-feet high—while hotly pursued by our star. Done hand-over-hand for real without benefit of either a safety net or airbags, the scene is framed in a single static longshot, allowing the two small climbing figures to become the sole focal points of the screen, and hence our eyes. Having both ascended to a narrow circular walkway ringing a cylindrical storage tank at its summit (one must only assume that the then still-rising superstar BD would have scoffed at the very idea of allow-

ing a stunt double to do his dirty work for him), the two men engage in a limited tussle while leaning precariously out over the safety-railing. One false step might well have meant curtains for either—or even *both*—of the participants! This vertigo-inducing elevated struggle ends when, thanks to an abrupt edit which interrupts the otherwise unbroken shot, BD punches the other "man" (i.e., a stiff dummy stand-in) over the edge, whereupon "he" plummets rigidly end over end to the ground below. (A similarly vertiginous "you are there"-dynamic can be felt during the climactic scenes atop a massive authentic industrial structure in director/star Robert Clarke's largely unsung but by no means forgotten made-by-the-skin-of-their-teeth *gringo* monster classic **THE HIDEOUS SUN DEMON** [1959, USA].)

Here seen with more hair than usual, masked wrestling movie genre fixture Carlos Suárez doesn't get much to do as one of Murayama's numerous henchmen (presumably it was a unionized operation and he had less seniority than the rest?). Disguised as

a nurse, *femme fatale* Barbara Angeli's mod "Mata Hari" Tania silences a bedridden hospital patient with a lethal injection. We also get babes with big bouffant hairdos in with-it mod ensembles, including miniskirts and capes, plus a would-be hitman with a glove that shoots bullets. In some cases within the broad Mexploitation spectrum, overuse of primary hues in the cinematography could often leave viewers not wearing sunglasses with either eyestrain or migraines (or both). In the present case, kooky komicbook kolor overkill only augments the movie's loopy alternate looniverse still further than the direction/music/editing (etc.) have already. For all its apparent *naïveté* of execution—but is it *really* as naïve as it seems to be?—there is a relentlessly reckless hyperactive energy to many scenes which makes them pop right off the screen and out into your living room with you. One can only wonder how exciting such images must have looked when screened ten or fifteen feet high at a theatrical venue. But who would need mind-altering substances for it? The *film itself* is enough of one! As if its very emulsion were

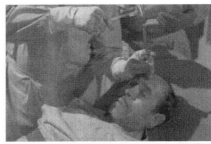

microencapsulated with raw hallucinogens which, when our brains scratch beneath its surface, are released via a kind of contact high into the viewer's very consciousness itself.

**BLUE DEMON CONTRA LOS CEREBROS INFERNALES**—which Urueta shot back-to-back with **BLUE DEMON CONTRA LAS DIABÓLICAS** ("*Blue Demon vs. The She-Devils*", 1968)—is for the most part briskly-paced, very cheaply constructed (this comes as no surprise, and is by *no* means necessarily a liability…and *definitely* not in this case) and contains enough oddball Crayola magic marker-hued stupidity/brilliance to be worth an informal perusal. This film can't quite hold a brainstem to Urueta's tremendous **EL BARÓN DEL TERROR** (a.k.a. **THE BRAINIAC**, 1961), but it's nice to see that the director's infatuations with wobbly Jell-O brains didn't end with that landmark Mexploitation masterpiece. Infectiously silly stuff, this… perfect for any brain-dead Mexi-*MONSTER!* maven (or *Weng's Chop*per, for that matter) to absorb into her/his psyche!

Urueta's next and final BD flick was **BLUE DEMON EN PASAPORTE DE LA MUERTE** ("*Blue Demon in Passport to Death*", 1967), which I've yet to see—but if it's anywhere even close to this much fun, sign me up!

*NOTE:* I found a fairly decent copy of **CERE-BROS INFERNALES**, slightly letterboxed (albeit with signs of video damage, clearly indicating that it was not mastered from a digital source) on the sell-through EastWest DVD label (issued in 2005). Unlike at least one other of their releases I have seen, which—surprise!—came complete with hard English subs, their print of **CEREBROS INFER-NALES** is presented strictly in its original Spanish. After dutifully watching my copy—which I picked up dirt-cheap (for around $3) at a Toronto bootleg/knock-off outlet—I discovered that my copy was incomplete. Three bucks might have been a real steal of a deal had my copy been complete. However, it ended cold at roughly around the 72-minute mark—right when the movie was gearing-up for its grand finale, yet! Assuming that this abrupt stoppage might merely be the fault of a fluke defective disc, I actually went back to the same "establishment"—*forget* asking for refunds at this joint!—and, sure enough, my second try with a new copy turned up exactly the same result (I should have just pocketed the sucker on the sly, but once again I shelled-out the full asking price, thinking it was well worth it). However, the movie merely cuts off then restarts right back at the beginning again without even so much as a pause or any dead air in-between. What a pisser! Luckily I still possessed an old VHS videotape copy I duped way back sometime in the '90s, so I could at least watch the end of it on that. But my final bit of advice to you is: see this sucker any way you can get it! But if you get a pain in your brain afterward, don't blame me…sometimes it just hurts so *good*, as the old song goes.

# PULAU PUTRI

("*Princess Island*")
1977, Indonesia. D: ???

**Reviewed by Steve Fenton**

Here's an obscure Indonesian comedic fantasy jungle adventure which I just happened across at YouTube recently purely by chance. Having done a search for it at the IMDb under the title given above, I have been unable to turn up any other info on it. Hence, this review is a bit more synopsis-heavy than I generally prefer, simply because of the film's obscurity value. Chances are, millions of words have already been written about it at thousands of 'blogs worldwide, but it's all new to me, so here goes nothin'…

Having suddenly come into possession of a treasure map along with an unexpected windfall, a down-on-his-luck schmoe—played by S. Bagyo, an unprepossessing diminutive, gap-toothed actor who very vaguely reminded me of a combination of Pinoy comedian Rene Requiestas and Hong Kong actor-producer Teddy Robin Kwan—goes off with two of his dorky buddies (evidently played by S. Diram and Dartu Helm) to a tropical jungle island in search of long-lost Japanese loot (possi-

bly left there during WW2?). Having become accidentally separated from his friends in the jungle, Bagyo, our unlikely hero, wanders about aimlessly and alone. Before you know it, he happens upon a group of beautiful women skinny-dipping in a pool at the foot of a waterfall (you can forget any nudity, 'cuz it ain't happening!). While spying on these bathers, he finds himself surrounded by more of the same Amazonian Asian tribeswomen, these ones clothed—surprisingly enough, in tailored yellow and red mini-dresses—and all pointing spears at him menacingly. When he makes a run through the jungle hoping to elude these apparently deadly females, they give chase. Thinking he has given them the slip, he winds up caught when the warrior women's leader loops her bullwhip around his neck, lassoing him. It develops that Bagyo's missing buddies have also been captured by the same warrior women, whose tribe are held in the sway of a hideous (and apparently immortal) spell-casting hag who lives in a cave in the area.

The silver-haired male tribal elder is clearly a much younger actor made-up to look about eighty-odd, but there is a reason for this, which is revealed later. There's also that creepy old hook-nosed, hunchbacked witch, who carries a snakehead walking stick and constantly cackles like Witchi-epoo (she even has a bubbling cauldron filled with noxious ingredients of indeterminate origin). After

the queen of the Amazons contemptuously slashes the witch with her whip, the hideous hag fatally blasts her assaulter with a crude green-and-red optical effect that shoots from the tip of her staff-*cum*-wand (**PULAU PUTRI**'s modest SFX highlight!). Cackling madly, while no one lifts a finger to prevent her, she then pursues Bagyo through the bush, making him her prisoner via magic and taking him back to her cave, evidently intent on cooking and eating him, as per your more common and garden variety fairy tale witch straight out of *Hansel and Gretel*. An obscure subplot entails Bagyo's two homely buds getting dolled-up in drag by the jungle girls, evidently intended to act as decoys in order to dupe the witch, who seems to be out to kill every young man in the vicinity (hence the temporary "sex-change" operation). When they discover a skeleton in the witch's cave—a decidedly flimsy set which, fittingly enough, looks like a hand-painted pantomime backdrop—Diram and Helm mistakenly believe the bleached bones to be the mortal remains of their missing friend. While escaping from the cave, curiously enough, the main hero also dons drag (much lame would-be comedy relief is derived from this tacky, overused gimmick). All three men are even uglier when seen dressed as women, but next to the witch with her gnarly prosthetic makeup, they're total babes! It turns out that the aforementioned "ancient" elder is in actuality only a young man in disguise after all, and has been wearing his phony grey facial hair and wig in hopes of pulling the wool over the witch-bitch's eyes as to his actual age. After the hero reveals his true identity, back to the witch's cave he goes as her prisoner. When he succeeds in stealing her walking stick while she sleeps, he thereafter turns the tables by making her his prisoner instead, and blows up her cave lair with the evil old bag's magic stick. He is hailed as a conquering hero by the tribespeople, and everybody mercilessly harangues and harasses the now-helpless hag, who goes up in supernatural flames at the end, her unnaturally-sustained existence ended at last. Although I could figure out most of the more simplistic aspects of the plot, the bizarre twist ending—which seems to involve some sort of retributory curse from beyond the grave (?)—quite frankly, eluded my grasp. A second "surprising" development following this further confused me.

While by no means anything overly special, **PU-LAU PUTRI** boasts a passably engaging oddball storyline and some relatively naturalistic—if sometimes too broad—performances from its trio of lead comics, who are likeable enough in a goofy way, and some of the easygoing comedy succeeds in registering even across the language barrier. That said, lowbrow "humor" definitely predominates. When combined with the film's more macabre elements, it makes for some rather grotesque visuals, central to which is the witch, natch. Adding some much-needed familiarity to this exceedingly foreign fare, some canned wolf-howls on the audio track are identical to those heard in Paul Naschy's *Waldemar Daninsky* series…but, most unfortunately, no werewolf shows up here! I was hoping at least one or two other more monstrous creatures might put in an appearance, but the creepy witch was the best this had to offer. Oh well, better than nothing, I suppose!

I recently came across a number of other lesser-covered Indonesian/Malaysian/Filipino (etc.) cinematic obscurities, and shall hopefully be reviewing some of those that fit *MONSTER!*'s stringent content guidelines in future issues.

*Note*: Just for the record, the cast also includes Eve Devi and Sol Saleh. Although many of the onscreen credits are given in English, no director is listed. Thanks go out to my Indonesian sister-in-law for verifying my translation of the title (ta, Henie)!

# TERROR FROM THE YEAR 5,000

**Reviewed by Steve Fenton**

Ad-line:
*"From Time Unborn… A Hideous She-Thing!"*

USA, 1958: D: Robert Gurney, Jr.

A pulp "penny dreadful" of the highest-lowest order, also written and produced by its director Robert J. Gurney, Jr., this was long one of the lesser-known and more elusive releases from American International Pictures' fruitful '50s Sci-fi cycle. Rather than being further confirmation of the old adage that the chase is better than the catch, this obscuriosity proves to be more than worth the long hunt.

It is introduced by a strident, echoey narrator's voice (e.g., "…Man struggles to penetrate the most imposing barrier of all: the time barrier!") which is still more emphatically over-dramatic than the norm even for a movie of this type from the same period (it makes those stentorian spoken intros heard on other films sound positively restrained by comparison). Further dating it, the script makes "topical" references to such Atomic Age concerns as uranium strikes and Geiger counters.

Nuclear physicist (what else?!) Professor Howard Erling (Frederic Downs) conducts experiments from his isolated mansion, located on an island somewhere in central Florida (the Everglades). Formerly employed in developing weapons technology by the U.S. Government, Prof. Erling had been accused of treason and left disgraced, then went into voluntary reclusion to conduct research of his own toward ends more beneficial to humanity. Via the time machine which they have invented and are still in the process of developing, Erling and his rich-kid junior assistant Victor (John Stratton) succeed in transporting back to the "present day" (*circa* the late-1950s) an abstract "humanoid female"-shaped statuette from far into the future. Through the process of carbon-dating (you mean it works *forwards*

**TERROR FROM THE YEAR 5,000**

JOYCE HOLDEN · WARD COSTELLO · FREDERIC DOWNS

Produced, Directed and Written by ROBERT J. GURNEY · A JAMES H. NICHOLSON and SAMUEL Z. ARKOFF Production · AN AMERICAN INTERNATIONAL PICTURE

too? Who knew!), this *objet d'art* is estimated to have been produced—despite what the movie's title claims!—in the year 5200, Anno Domini. Much like **TERROR FROM THE YEAR 5000** itself, some might concur (and indeed have), that this female figurine shouldn't even exist at all...but here it is, for what it's worth. Put under chemical and other analyses, the statuette is discovered to be intensely radioactive. Having had the confounding object sent to him and been left baffled as to its metallurgical makeup and origin, Dr. Bob Hodges (Ward Costello) journeys to Erling's isolated lab for an explanation to this mystery.

Subsequent experimentation with the inter-time cabinet transports a living organism—in the form of a small four-eyed, cat-like mammalian—back from the future. In the interests of communicating information back and forth between the present and future, together with their unknown (human?) contact far ahead in the Fifth Millennium, using their two-way time machine the 20th century scientists begin "trading" mundane contemporary objects for their futuristic equivalents. During the course of this "getting to know you" interaction, Prof. Erling and Dr. Hodges receive a cryptic encoded message which translates to "Save us", amounting to a collective SOS call from Mankind's time-lost descendants. Eager to make progress in their ongoing experiments with the machine, the overzealous Victor

unwisely messes about with the transmitting hardware, unwittingly bringing *something* back that is very much alive...and highly lethal. Having been the one who had earlier been responsible--unbeknownst to his colleagues—for conducting the unauthorized experiment which had brought back that multi-eyed cat-thing, Victor had secretly disposed of the dead creature by enclosing it in a container and sinking it to the bottom of a nearby bayou.

Upon being burned by radiation, Victor subsequently flees hospitalization in order to obsessively continue furthering his illicit experiments back at the Erling house. Overloading the equipment when he cranks up the power to full-blast, Victor brings a ferocious screeching female subhumanoid with hideously deformed facial features back to our time. Complete with shiny fingernails which can induce hypnosis, "she" (played by Salome Jens) is rendered "invisible" via a scintillating/coruscating sequined body-suit (foreshadowing **PREDATOR**'s famous camouflaging technique). The creature murders a nurse and, thanks to a special latex mask, "steals" the dead woman's face in order to assume her identity and thus remain incognito while moving amongst us. Due to Earth's human inheritors having been left mutated following nuclear Armageddon, the she-creature has been dispatched from 5200 A.D. by others of her kind to seek "new blood with undamaged, pre-atomic genes", which will be

Salome Jens as the shapely if facially hideous she-monster from the future prowls the lab in
**TERROR FROM THE YEAR 5000**

used to repopulate the ravaged future world. When unmasked, the mutant reveals her true self, thus propelling the closing concatenation.

**TERROR FROM THE YEAR 5000** ends with an inspirational moral message which is as pertinent today in these times of unchecked genetic tampering as it was back in the days of rampant atomic paranoia: "The future is what we make it. Whether there will be creatures like her depends on *us*. All of us—on Mankind."

Complete with a frequent laboratory setting, the film's shrill, shrieking melodramatic musical score sounds like it might well have been lifted from a '40s Monogram Pictures or Producers Releasing Corporation horror cheapie. A red herring creepy handyman who lives in a rude shack whose walls are pasted with cheesecake pin-ups recalls a similar character seen in David Kramarsky's **THE BEAST WITH 1,000,000 EYES!** (USA, 1955). In a typical example of AIP self-promotion, the billboards of an "incidental" movie theater seen onscreen in the present film loudly advertise the company's then-concurrent and much better known SF/horror schlocker **I WAS A TEENAGE FRANKENSTEIN** (USA, 1958). I'm not 100% positive if the present movie is extant on DVD anywhere, but I managed to download myself a watchably murky old videotape dupe of it from an online torrent site via Vuze…*au gratis*,

you might say (ain't this so-called "file-sharing" shit a wonderful thing?!). But rest assured that I would buy a legit copy in a heartbeat if I ever ran across one, so don't hold it against me.

This film's rating at the IMDb is a mere "2.3" on the Sphincter Scale. Don't listen to 'em and their lowest-common-denominator bull-crap! Trust me—it's a lot better than that. If you're someone who appreciates old school sci-fi/monster flicks made with some real imagination on an absolute pittance, by all means give this one a spin. You might laugh at it sometimes; you might well even sneer at it contemptuously upon occasion…but there is just no way you can *hate* it. If you do, there's no hope for you, I'm afraid. You have been warned.

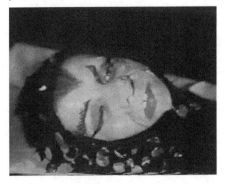

# THE BEAST WITH 1,000,000 EYES!

**Reviewed by Steve Fenton**

USA, 1955. D: David Kramarsky

Co-produced by director David Kramarsky, Roger Corman and James H. Nicholson—the latter of whom reportedly coined the fanciful title (one which was, quite frankly, impossible for its puny budget to even come *close* to living up to!)—this notorious-if-endearing '50s lo-fi sc-fi schlocker was made for American Releasing Corporation (ARC), immediate forerunner of the much-more-famous American International Pictures (AIP), which Nicholson went on to form with his future long-time business partner Samuel Z. Arkoff.

This present title represented the movie debut of largely unsung D.I.Y. monster-maker Paul Blaisdell (1930-1983), whose clunky, floppy foam-rubbery creations are fondly remembered by legions of psychotronic movie enthusiasts. Looking to hire a special effects man for as cheaply as possible on **BEAST**, the penny-pinching, cost- and corner-cutting Corman approached future *Famous Monsters of Filmland* editor Forrest J. Ackerman for suggestions. When wunderkind stop-motion animation wiz Ray Harryhausen proved well beyond the reach of the present film's exceedingly meager finances—Corman's total FX budget had originally been a mere $200 [!], which he subsequently and grudgingly doubled [!!]—the producers ultimately settled on Blaisdell, who had then been working as an illustrator (including artworks for *Spaceway*, an SF magazine) while moonlighting in other capacities. He fabricated the titular—only *two*-eyed!—rather too-cuddly-looking beast in the form of an 18"-tall puppet, which appeared onscreen for mere

seconds at the climax of the film, and even then was further obscured by the optical superimposition of a giant transparent "alien" eye atop it. He also built the alien's miniature spaceship, which didn't remotely match with the "life-size" mock-up craft jerry-rigged out of various bits of junk (including mufflers from Model-T Fords) by ARC's poverty-stricken prop department. Both the miniature and full-scale versions of the spacecraft were subsequently thrown back on the scrapheap, whereupon Blaisdell built another "all-new" mini version which sees only minimal usage in the finished film—blink twice and you'll miss it, much like the monster itself, which would be difficult to get a good look at even if you happened to have a million eyes of your own, all with perfect 20/20 vision.

What about the plot, you may be wondering? Everyman farmer Alan (Paul Birch, probably best known by most '50s cult schlock cinema fans as the predatory humanoid alien of Corman's **NOT OF THIS EARTH** [USA, 1957]) struggles to make a going concern of his failing family ranch. Not only is his professional life suffering for it, but his personal one as a result, too, with he and his dissatisfied neurotic wife Carol (Lorna Thayer) involved in a dysfunctional and rapidly disintegrating marriage. This state of affairs understandably also adversely affects the couple's teenage daughter Sandy (Dona Cole), who is engaged in an ongoing domestic dispute with her mother. Middle-aged and plagued with bitterness and regret over all his lost chances and what might have been but isn't, **BEAST** opens with the Birch character's literate, if pensively-narrated, philosophical ruminations. Set in a bleak, desolate and dehydrated rural landscape ("a perfect place to hatch a brood of horror", muses Birch's ominously grumbling voiceover), the surrounding arid wasteland ever encroaches on the boundaries of the farming family's isolated oasis of civilization ("We might as well be on another planet").

The sudden, ear-piercingly high-pitched whine of something unseen passing overhead (yes, it's a UFO) not only shatters the overlying mood of somnolent if faintly sinister tranquility, but also Mom's coffee pot, household glassware and window panes, as well. A blatant symbol of the family's deteriorating home life and rather reminiscent of poltergeist

activity, this impromptu destruction in their home externalizes the inner turmoil of Thayer as Carol, the chronically depressive wife and matriarch of the terminally stressed family unit. Constantly teetering on the brink of a nervous breakdown, in one scene she goes into a hysterical tizzy when she burns her precious apple pie. Further emphasizing how their world is falling apart while showing that our protagonists are being attacked from both outside as well as from within, in a subsequent scene which neatly foreshadows Alfred Hitchcock's **THE BIRDS** (USA, 1963), Birch is beset by a fluttering flock of enraged blackbirds.

An extraterrestrial spacecraft has touched down to Earth in an arroyo adjacent to the farmlands. Within the craft resides a malevolent non-human entity

(i.e., Blaisdell's fleetingly glimpsed puppet monster). Interestingly enough, in the original script—which bears only a passing resemblance to the finished product—the puppet monster was presented as an enslaved pawn of the title beast (aforementioned all-seeing "million"-eyeball), although this rather "subliminal" plot point is not clarified in the film itself, other than for the fact that the scarcely shown puppet can be seen wearing shackles around the wrists of its clawed arms, implying its captive and subservient status. Most viewers will likely just assume that Blaisdell's monster—both a figurative as well as quite literal puppet—is the titular beast, and such a distinction is of little real import anyway, considering its brief appearance. That said, while physical monsters come few and far between here, the omnipresent influence of the alien beast saturates the very emulsion of the film itself, and can be felt ever lurking at the edges of the frame throughout the running time.

Former Silent Era comedian Chester Conklin (**BEAST**'s recognizable "name" guest star) plays a neighboring rancher whose ordinarily amiable milking cow unexpectedly turns ornery; this due to being "possessed" by some as-yet unknown outside influence (as in outside our known world as well as beyond our ken). In a subsequent scene, the family's Rin Tin Tin-like guard dog Duke, due to his

having had a close encounter of the third kind with the alien presence, goes against his normally protective if non-aggressive nature by turning vicious. It is during such scenes of "ferocious" fauna (described in the dialogue as an "animal revolution") that the budgetary limitations—including a distinct lack of wranglers/trainers—are most apparent; as when his mad cow "savagely attacks" Conklin and flapping, clucking "killer" chickens are flung bodily at Mom from out of frame (possibly even by Mr. Corman himself [?]).

All this animalistic adversity eventually causes Thayer's matriarchal protagonist to re-evaluate her feelings for her alienated kinfolk, narrowing the void which yawns between them as broad and unfathomable as outer space. Ultimately, the formerly fractured and fragmented clan pulls together as one to oppose the evil alien force, which proves powerless against the combined might of their familial love. Don't all groan at once.

Although critically underfunded—a state of affairs which has proven by no means always a liability in the cinema—THE BEAST WITH 1,000,000 EYES! has a nicely authentic down-home country/grass roots feel. Optically-printed superimposed spirals, spacey humming sound FX, a giant eyeball (of *course*!) and that peek at Blaisdell's puppet beast all join forces in a seeming attempt to undermine things, all to no avail. For me, at least—if not teeming millions of others—*something* about this film has always clicked in my mind. I can't quite put my finger on it specifically, but it works for me, and I'm glad it does.

A deaf-mute voyeuristic pervert seen here—known ominously only as "Him" (Leonard Tarver)—is a virtual carbon copy of a character in Robert J. Gurney, Jr.'s TERROR FROM THE YEAR 5000 (USA, 1958). Prone to "reading" girly magazines in a dismal shack wall-papered with cheesecake pin-ups, Him plays peeping tom on teenybopper Cole as Birch's precocious daughter while she enjoys a not-so-skinny dip down at the local swimming hole.

Interestingly enough, the lonely, aurally/vocally challenged Him character, treated with little empathy or tolerance by his human neighbors in the film, is as marginalized and alienated as the title E.T. invader, under whose dominant thrall Him falls because he is so simple-minded and thus easier to control, as with the other "lower life-forms" which the beast uses against us. This latter thematic detail provided the convenient rationale for the film's gross overstatement of a title: that, rather than actually possessing a million eyes of its own, it instead saw through those ocular organs of the various teeming species of wildlife surrounding it. But even if you

do suspend your disbelief and accept that imaginative "cheat" explanation, a pooch, a moo-cow and a dozen or two feathered flappers still falls somewhat short of a million in the eyeball department.

During its original theatrical run, *Variety*'s reviewer levelled such unflattering adjectives as "tedious" and "confusing" at the film. In a long-overdue retrospective of Paul Blaisdell's modest but historically notable career, for his article entitled "Hollywood's Forgotten Monster-Maker" in *Cinefantastique* magazine (Vol. 20, #5, May 1990), Randy Palmer wrote: "Undoubtedly, the best thing about THE BEAST WITH 1,000,000 EYES! is the title", also rather unfairly describing it as "sheer torture to endure". While generally reviled as a bad joke by the relatively few who have ever seen it, the film is by no means as awful as you might have been led to expect. So don't believe what you've heard, use a little imagination to fill in the blanks instead of expecting ultra-realistic presentation to do all your imagining

**The following is an excerpt from the 1978 interview with Paul Blasidell that appeared in Tim Paxton's "Photo Fiends" magazine #3:**

PHOTO FIENDS: *Was Roger Corman's THE BEAST WITH 1,000,000 EYES! The first film you did SFX for? How large was "The Beast"?*

PAUL BLAISDELL: Yes, that was the first one I ever did any effects for, painful as it was. Frankly, I think he *[Ed: Corman]* got exactly what he wanted. I wish it *[Ed: i.e., "The Beast"]* had been photographed better and used differently, but...THE BEAST WITH 1,000,000 EYES! was the devil-like bat creature that was going to shoot Paul Birch with a ray-gun before Paul plugged him with a 30-30 Winchester. He was not "The Beast with a Million Eyes"! I think at the time most everybody at American International Pictures *[Ed: then still known as American Releasing Corporation]*, including Roger Corman, liked the miniatures, the mock-up spaceship hull and the animated creatures and the rocket ship miniature that took off from the desert; but somehow it seemed to lose something in the presentation, the photography was off and the story didn't quite carry the continuity. So I'm afraid most of that ended up on the cutting room floor.

How large was "Little Hercules"? – Well, he was built to be 18 inches tall, about one quarter life-size.

Screaming Terror!

THE BEAST WITH 1,000,000 EYES!

filmed for WIDE SCREEN in TERROR-SCOPE

with Paul BIRCH · Lorna THAYER · Dona COLE and the BEAST

Produced & Directed by DAVID KRAMARSKY · Screenplay by TOM FILER
A SAN MATEO PICTURE · Presented by PALO ALTO PRODUCTIONS

for you, and maybe—just *maybe*, mind you—you might derive even half as much benefit from this humble offering as I did when I first saw it 20-odd years ago, and still do whenever I re-watch it. You never can tell—stranger things have happened!

Not bad at all, really, considering the whole thing from start to finish cost less than $25,000 (a critically pitiful price-tag even for the time in which it was made). As was the modus operandi of the guy who made way more than a hundred movies

in Hollywood and never (well, *barely* ever) lost a dime, **BEAST** definitely accomplished its objective in its producers' eyes by recouping its initial cash outlay numerous-fold. However, because he felt that director Kramarsky did such a piss-poor job on the present film—many elements of which got botched during production—Corman himself opted to both produce and direct ARC's admittedly better next monster opus, **DAY THE WORLD ENDED** (USA, 1955), also co-starring Birch. And the rest, as they say, is history.

## THE MEMORY BANK

Here is a sketch from memory of Paul Blaisdell's Lil' Hercules, a creature that has always occupied a shelf in my mind's bookcase of cool stuff. The first time I saw this film was on late night TV back in the early '70s—WEWS CHANNEL 8 Cleveland, OH. I must have been around 11 or so, but I never found the film dull or stupid. The notion of an all-encompassing mind force fascinated me. I knew the film was going to be on TV a few days in advance so I scraped together some cash and bought a 50-ft. roll of Super 8mm film. I set up my camera and carefully caught brief instances of the plot including (and man, did I have to wait and make sure I had enough film left in the camera) the appearance of Blaisdell's critter and the spaceship taking off. ~ *Tim Paxton*

# Return to NUKE 'EM HIGH
# VOL. 1

**Reviewed by Brian Harris**

2013, USA. D: Lloyd Kaufman

Not sure about everybody else, but I for one am shocked that Troma has finally made their first sequel to **CLASS OF NUKE 'EM HIGH** (1986) after all of these ye— what's that you say? There already were sequels made? Two of them, you say? Yeah…let me rephrase that: I for one am shocked that Troma has finally made their first *good* sequel to **CLASS OF NUKE 'EM HIGH** after all of these years. See how I did that there? Conversational snark and positivity… now that's high-class writin'. Honestly, Troma has always been hit-or-miss for me; there are times when the kitchen sink approach to low-budget filmmaking and a healthy dose of juvenile potty humor is just what the doctor ordered, and there are times when

it's flat-out exhausting. Much respect to **THE TOX-IC AVENGER** (1984) and **CLASS OF NUKE 'EM HIGH**, but I wasn't really interested in rediscovering the sleazy wonders of Troma until their release of **POULTRYGEIST: NIGHT OF THE CHICKEN DEAD** (2006) and **FATHER'S DAY** (2011), as well as their acquisition of Drew Bolduc's **THE TAINT** (2010). I wouldn't say I'm a diehard Troma fan now, but I'm much more willing to give Lloyd & Co.'s newer productions the benefit of the doubt.

Which brings us to: **RETURN TO NUKE 'EM HIGH VOL.1**. The volume designation—unsubstantiated rumors claim Quentin Tarantino suggested Kaufman go all **KILL BILL** with this newest—means there's more to the story than what's presented

ANCHOR BAY FILMS presents a LLOYD KAUFMAN and MICHAEL HERZ TROMA TEAM production
**CATHERINE CORCORAN and ASTA PAREDES**
**FIGHT BULLIES AND DEFEND THEIR DUCK BABY LOVE CHILD WITH A SUPERDUPER HI-POWERED LASER in**

then…"TO BE CONTINUED". No resolutions of any kind, the film feels pointless. That said, it's funny (and sexy) as hell.

Everything you expect from a Troma film (i.e., masturbation, fat people, nudity, lipstick lesbians, farting, a manic Lloyd Kaufman and pollution) is on display, so if you know what you're getting into beforehand it works brilliantly. However, as I mentioned above, the film goes nowhere as there's no real resolution (natch!). The film doesn't even begin to build steam until the final quarter and by that time you're wondering where it's all going. You won't find out. To some that's a good reason to avoid this film but I say, *go for it*. Enjoy yourself with what little story you get here and cross those fingers and hope that we do indeed get a Volume 2, because this film would make a terrible standalone.

A couple things I loved about **RETURN TO NUKE 'EM HIGH VOL.1** were the FX—which are pure gloppy, gross goodness—and the wild and wildly inappropriate, score. Some people may disagree with me on this but I noticed a real step forward in terms of Lloyd's filmmaking abilities and the writing quality. A few well-placed cuts and this could easily receive "mainstream" indie appeal, as it had some smart, subtle, artistic moments. *Yeah, right.* And where would that be…sandwiched between the dog murder, duck rape and lesbian lovemaking?! Seriously, I found it to be a bit smarter than expected. Not sure who deserves the pat on the back for that, though, as five people are credited as writers or story contributors on this production.

here. I feel that's worth mentioning as the film *literally* goes nowhere.

Allow me to break it down, break it down…

After the events that transpired in **CLASS OF NUKE 'EM HIGH**, the high school is rebuilt and the Tromaville Nuclear Plant is long gone, now replaced by an even deadlier new antagonist…*THE TROMAVILLE TROMORGANIC PLANT*. No longer does nuclear power send collective shivers down the spine, now the world fears non-organic and genetically modified foodstuffs! Eeeek!

When school lunch tacos soaked in chemicals are served to the students of Tromaville High School, all hell breaks loose and the once-nerdy Glee Club are transformed into snarling, murderous, makeup-sporting *Cretins*! Their only purpose is to maim, murder and destroy everything in their path—but their reign of terror doesn't go unchallenged, as two adorable lesbian lovers transform into ruthless vigilantes sporting a pregnant tummy and a massive penis. And…that's pretty much about it. We get unlikely friends, polluted tacos, transformations, Cretins, lesbian avengers and

If you're wondering whether this film has monsters, it does, though they're in the form of mutants. From the look of the original art poster for this film—probably before it was split into two films—they intended to feature full-on mutated creatures, but no such luck,

so they're likely on the way for Volume 2. Until then you'll have to be satisfied with a hot lesbian sporting a tree limb-sized dong that eats hearts. If I didn't know better I'd say that Kaufman was going for Oscar® gold with this sucker!

I actually planned to purchase this film on Blu-ray disc, but now I'll be holding off on doing so until the next installment is completed.

# COMING SOON FROM ANCHOR BAY FILMS

# TRACK OF THE MOON BEAST

Reviewed by Douglas Waltz

USA, 1976. D: Dick Ashe
*Written by Bill Finger & Charles Sinclair*
*Starring Chase Cordell, Leigh Drake,*
*Gregorio Sala & Patrick Wright*

Paul Carlson (Chase Cordell) is out in the desert digging up ancient artifacts when his old teacher, Johnny Longbow (Gregorio Sala), surprises him with a couple students in tow and the lovely, Kathy Nolan (Leigh Drake), who hits it off immediately with Paul. He drags her off to his favorite spot in the desert so she can get some shots of the full moon. Meanwhile, a meteor has struck the surface of the moon, sending fragments to Earth in the form of micro-meteors. Sure enough, one of those flies by Paul and Kathy and manages to imbed a small fragment in Paul's skull. Now, when the moon is full the fragment triggers a change in Paul and he becomes a reptilian monster hinted about in an ancient Indian legend.

**TRACK OF THE MOON BEAST** wants to be a different take on the whole lunar monster thing. By blending Indian legend with the effects the moon has on the surface of the earth, the idea is sound. Unfortunately, the execution is a little overbearing.

Our two leads, Chase Cordell and Leigh Drake, never managed to go on to do much else in the realm of acting, and this is horribly apparent, especially in the case of Ms. Drake. Her delivery of her lines is awful. And her relationship with Paul is unbelievable, in that it just sort of happens. One minute they are introduced to each other, the next they are doing the lip-lock/dance of love. And when they kiss, you need to back up: I would be amazed if neither of them chipped a tooth! And this happens several times in the flick.

This is one of those movies that could really do well with a rerelease if they could find a longer version. The film is filled with gore effects that are just mere flashes on the screen. The scene where the lizard monster attacks a group of guys playing poker in a tent has an arm being ripped off, but it cuts away really quickly. The movie actually sat on a shelf for four years and then went right to television, so cuts had to be made. With zero nudity or profanity, this is probably the only cut of the film that exists. It got a second wind of sorts during the VHS boom with a box cover that was infinitely better than the movie contained within.

The most recognizable actor in the bunch has to be Patrick Wright. As I saw the sheriff of the town, I immediately flashed to **BENEATH THE VALLEY OF THE ULTRA VIXENS** (1979) and his scenes with Kitten Natividad. Luckily, he keeps his clothes on in this film, but the frequent shoulder-fondling he gives to Johnny Longbow in any scene they share made me feel uncomfortable.

But, this is *MONSTER!*...we all want to know about the monster, right? Well, makeup man Joe Blasco, who gave us the cool effects in David Cronenberg's **RABID** (1977), does produce a pretty nice rubber suit. There are movements that give away the rubber suit, but it was 1976. We knew it was a guy in a suit. It actually was Blasco in the suit—a good idea because he knew what it could and couldn't do. The face is especially creepy. Because it's the moon that triggers the transformation and the suit appears to be black, it is hard to see in a lot of the scenes, but they do have a slow dissolve effect that takes place in the hospital where we get a better look at it. This also might be the only movie where they lock up the monster, and then it transforms and doesn't escape! Instead he just wakes up the next morning strapped down with the realization of what he has become.

I did expect better from the writing team that gave us the superior **GREEN SLIME** (1968). At least Bill Finger has gone on to a lucrative career in writing Batman video games, while this was Charles Sinclair's swansong. Director Dick Ashe really gave it his all, as this is the only feature he ever directed.

And when they decide to kill the monster, it is just done. There is no long hunt-down-the-monster montage. They just shoot him with an arrow that has a moon-rock arrowhead. Apparently it triggers a meltdown and turns Paul into a pile of ash. And then the movie is done. No ending credits. Nothing. Just fade to black with Johnny Longbow standing in the desert next to a pile of ash that was once his friend.

**TRACK OF THE MOON BEAST** has the awesome nugget of an idea that fails in the execution. Maybe if it had seen a theatrical release with all of the special effects intact, we might have something better. I want to believe that…but then Leigh

The Rising Moon Creates a Monster

Drake does what she thinks is acting and it pains me a little.

The monster, however, is pretty cool.

# CREATURE FEATURE

## Monthly MONSTER! Column by Louis Paul

*Vampires who must be halted by being urinated on, female ghosts who return from the dead to avenge their untimely death via sexual predators, demons from the netherworld who seek carnal delights from beyond the grave, skin-peelers who believe the flesh of young females will make wonderful lanterns, slimy insects placed in unmentionable orifices by leering demented wizards...these are just a few of the Asian monster types to be found in Chinese films.*

I've seen quite a few such movies in a nearly decade-long, exhausting review of hundreds of Hong Kong and mainland-lensed features. Most of the films I viewed were made in a period between the mid-'70s and 1997. That was the year that Hong Kong was returned to Chinese rule (from the British), and a tightening over cinematic subject matter by Communist authorities on the Chinese mainland appeared as a result.

I became fascinated with what appeared to me to be an almost complete disregard for genre film aesthetics, as often a single film will have comedic elements and a heavy dollop of sensuality, via many scenes of simulated sex, graphic bloodletting—and in some, cinematic evidence of the filmmaker's insanity, if we are judging by Western standards.

Hong Kong cinema really fascinated me. I felt like I was slowly embarking on a path towards an unknown destination, never sure where I would end up. I enjoyed the action films quite a lot, and found it quite interesting as flying fists and feet eventually gave way to two-fisted guns. Even some of the comedies were not as alien to me as I feared, and I enjoyed them despite at times feeling like an outsider, being a non-Asian from the West.

The horror films and thrillers—that's another story entirely. In most cases, I've seen films I never want to view again...*ever*...for a variety of reasons. Mostly, because I've experienced something which, once seen, can never be un-seen. But in hindsight that was all part of the excitement of the discovery for me. Seeing something I've never seen before...the experience.

If something I've written here will entertain you enough to entice you to want to track down some of these films, then I've done a good job. I'm not sure of any of the UE and Tai Seng video shops

I haunted so long ago are even in existence anymore—or if some of these films can even be found—but I'm sure if there's a will...there's a way. Happy haunting!

# A BITE OF LOVE

(*Yi yau O.K.* / *"One Bite O.K."*)
HK, 1990. D: Stephen Shin Gei-yin
*Cast: George Lam Chi-cheung, Rosamund Kwan Chi-lam, Norman Chu (Tsui Siu-keung)*

George Lam Chi-cheung stars as a (Western) version of a vampire. Infected by a European bloodsucker (the Dracula-type), Lam Chi-cheung cannot seem to have

Ghost Story Of
Kam Pin Mui

too becomes a vampire. The film then follows both men as they attempt to lure Rosamund Kwan into the darkness and a life as a vampire, for she was born with a special type of blood that will make the winner, the "King of Vampires".

There are few films in the HK horror pantheon that use the motif of Westernized vampires (think of Dracula with the flowing cape). More often than not, it is the *jiangshi* (a.k.a. *gyonshi*, etc.)—the hopping vampires dressed in ritual costumes who seem slow and easy to kill but are really deadly—that we are familiar with when thinking of vampires in the context of the Chinese cinema. Along with **DR. VAMPIRE** (1990) and **ROMANCE OF THE VAMPIRES** (1994), this is one of the few films to feature the idea of the Western vampire in the Eastern horror tradition. Unfortunately, it is the least entertaining of the three, due to a lack of charismatic acting by all of the main players.

# GHOST STORY OF KAM PUI MUI

(*Liao zhai Jin Ping Mei*)
HK/Thailand, 1991. D: Bo Han Li
*Cast: Chin Lin, Han Chi, McLaren Wu, Wu Ma, Chan Pui- ki*

normal relations with people, including the romantic interest played by Rosamund Kwan, and finds himself raiding the local blood banks to satisfy his bloody cravings. When the supply runs dry, he must decide if he is ready, willing, and able to kill in order to continue to exist. Norman Chu is a Triad gang leader who is in desperate need of a cure for his illness; when he receives a transfusion of Lam Chi-cheung's blood, he

Chin Lin (McLaren Wu) is the daughter of a prostitute; her sister—named Pink!—has already been sold to a hideous madam named Aunt Chui, and Chin Lin dreads being sold off into a forced life as a prostitute at the same brothel. When a kindly suitor comes to town to rescue Chin Lin, and finds that she has been sold to Aunt Chui, he is beaten and stoned to death. The suitor returns from the dead as Chin Lin's protector, forever professing his love for her. However, Chin Lin must learn the ways to please Aunt Chui's clientele, and with her more adept sister Pink as a teacher, she throws herself completely into her work. At night, the suitor's ghost comes to visit Chin Lin, and this is the time where she can become vulnerable and share her love. Unfortunately, Aunt Chui learns of the ghostly visits and hires an evil priest to eradicate the good spirit of the suitor.

A strange, sometimes compelling romance with a startling amount of gratuitous nudity, this film attempts to cover similar territory as that of the financially successful *Erotic Ghost Story* series, but comes off as more mean-spirited fare, with touches of a bittersweet romance at its edges. For those looking for a more (*ahem*) literal kind of thrill, there's ample nudity on view from star McLaren Wu.

# THE OCCUPANT

*Ling qi bi ren* / "*Spirit Compels People*")
HK, 1984. D: Ronnie Yu Yan-tai
Cast: Chow Yun-fat, Sally Yeh (Yip Sin-man), Raymond Wong Bak-ming, Melvin Wong Kam-sum, Lo Lieh, Judy Li

A Canadian student (Sally Yeh) comes to Hong Kong to do research, but she moves into the wrong vacated apartment. A female singer who had been involved in a fatal romantic triangle decades past died there and, slowly, her spirit begins to possess Sally. Chow Yun-fat co-stars as a policeman who takes a romantic interest in Yeh, and Raymond Wong is a sleazy realtor who also fancies her for himself. In little time, Yeh becomes possessed **EXORCIST**-style and is bouncing both men off the walls.

This is a curious and not completely successful entry into the HK ghost film genre. Although peopled by good actors and directed by Ronnie Yu, a man with a great cinematic eye, all are let down by an insipid and poorly-constructed script. Film producer Raymond Wong makes an occasional appearance in films in goofy, nebbish sort of roles. Here, he does more of the same, but rises to the occasion when both he and Chow must get deadly serious as Yeh starts to levitate and becomes extremely deadly. At the film's climax, the evil spirit is exorcised from Yeh's body, but a slightly comical freeze-frame reveals that it has returned to possess her.

# SEEDING OF A GHOST

(*Zhong gui* / "*Seed Ghost*")
HK, 1983. Ds: Phillip Ko-fei, Yang Chuan, Norman Chu (Tsui Siu-keung)
Cast: Phillip Ko-fei, Norman Chu (Tsui Siu-keung), Chaun Chi-hui, Yu Chi-wai

A taxi driver with an extremely unfaithful wife continues his day-to-day existence, vaguely aware of his wife's cheating ways. When the wife learns that she is pregnant and goes to her latest suitor with the news, he rejects her violently. As she walks the night in despair, a gang of psychotic male thugs gang-rape her and as she attempts escape, the woman falls to her death. The mourning husband learns of her death, and then, with the aid of a wizard (a slightly odd one at that), he places a curse on all those he holds responsible for her death. The husband and wizard experiment on the wife's corpse in an extremely bizarre manner, culminating with a touch of necrophilia. Everyone from the youths who attacked her to her suitors become victims in an elaborate and gory plan of revenge.

The above synopsis does not come anywhere near to conveying the extreme and distasteful atmosphere in which this film is soaked. While it contains enough nudity in its first half to satisfy leering Category III fans, the rest of it is a gore-fueled journey into a dimension of the absurd. Cast members vomit worms and insects, body

SEEDING OF A GHOST

# WIZARD'S CURSE

(*Yau guai du shi* / "*Demon Big City*")
HK, 1992. D: Yuen Cheung-yan
*Cast: Ellen Chan Ar-lun, Lam Ching-ying, Cheung Kwok-keung, Billy Chow Bei-lei, Mimi Chu Mi-mi, Woo Fung, Charlie Cho Cha-lei, Yeung Cheung-yan*

**Thai poster for WIZARD'S CURSE**

The film begins in Thailand, where two ghostly spirits that also happen to be sexually obsessed vampires are vanquished by a Taoist Monk (Lam Ching-ying). Afterward, an evil wizard revives them, and they travel to Hong Kong seeking out Lam Ching-ying and any of his descendants, which, in this case, turns out to be his sole heir, his virginal daughter. HK cop Cheung Kwok-keung lusts after Ching-ying's daughter but also seeks to aid her against the malicious spirits. As the trio does battle against the deadly duo from the netherworld, there is only one way that Ching-ying's daughter can be saved; she must make love with Cheung Kwok-keung, and their union will contribute to the defeat of the eerie duo.

parts inflate with grue-filled pus, then explode in a spectacular manner. Finally, at the climax, the wife of the last suitor is celebrating a special occasion when a tentacled creature causes havoc and all hell breaks loose. Of all the HK horror films, this is one of the most extreme. Not for the squeamish!

Scripted by the one-and-only Wong Jing, this one is a mess from start to finish, but, like the best Wong Jing productions, it's a film that is hilariously funny in parts, and deliriously strange in others. On occasion, it has a slight erotic charge, some decent action scenes, and a quirky storyline that has to be seen to be believed.

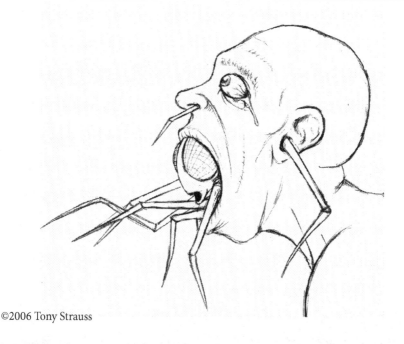

# My First Monster!

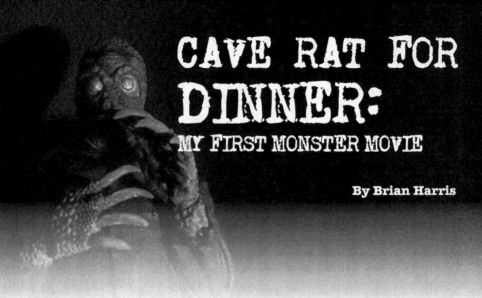

# CAVE RAT FOR DINNER:
## MY FIRST MONSTER MOVIE

### By Brian Harris

On many occasions in my writings I've discussed my upbringing—essentially cable television was my nanny—and my mother's love for all things horror, so I won't rehash. Suffice it to say, it's no surprise I'm as dedicated to horror, sci-fi and fantasy cinema as I am. It's not a hobby or distraction for me; it's an integral part of who I am.

Surprisingly, I can recall the first film that truly scared me (**DOMINIQUE**, 1979), but I'm at a complete loss when it comes to my first monster movie. My earliest memory—I'm thinking I was probably around the age of 3 years old—is of the 1956 feature, **THE MOLE PEOPLE**. As you can imagine, it's hard for me to say how I felt while watching, but it obviously left an impression on me. Some of the other "monster movies" I remember seeing as a young child include **CREATURE FROM THE BLACK LAGOON** (1954), **THE TIME MACHINE** (1960), **JOURNEY TO THE CENTER OF THE EARTH** (1959), **THE WAR OF THE GARGANTUAS** (1966), **THEM!** (1954), **KINGDOM OF THE SPIDERS** (1977), **THE FOOD OF THE GODS** (1976), **EMPIRE OF THE ANTS** (1977), Ray Harryhausen's *Sinbad* films, **JASON AND THE ARGONAUTS** (1963), and **THE LOST WORLD** (1960). Hell, one of my favorites is Roger Corman's mutant sleazefest, **HUMANOIDS FROM THE DEEP** (1980).

Today everything is pretty much lumped together under the general label of "horror films" and the traditional monster movie is nearly extinct—though some do still pop up. Not to generalize, but modern horror fans seem obsessed only with brutality and torture, seeing the nastiest of the nasty in order to add to their "metal" street cred. *"Dude, A SERBIAN FILM bothered you?!! I saw it six*

*times and wasn't in the slightest bit disturbed! They didn't go far ENOUGH!"* What happened to the fun? Must there always be chest-beating and dick measuring? Hell, just give me a man-eating snow beast and call it a day.

*And fer Christ's sake would you put your dick back!*

Before some of you start wondering when I'm going to log off the computer at the old folks' home and get down off of the soapbox, don't get it twisted—I love gruesome gore and mind-bending mayhem just as much as the next guy. I can go from watching **REVENGE OF THE CREATURE** (in 3-D no less!) to **FACES OF DEATH** without skipping a beat. I just yearn to see giant ants, mutant rats and rampaging rubber suits once again receive the love and respect they deserve. I'm betting Tim feels the same way, which is why we're seeing *Monster!* and *Monster! International* rise from the literary swamps.

Those of you that haven't been privileged enough (*snicker*) to have seen **THE MOLE PEOPLE**, don't break a leg running to check it out: *IT DID NOT HOLD UP WELL.* The albinos look like mimes, Hugh Beaumont will always be Ward Cleaver and the mole people themselves resemble a cross between The Gillman from **THE CREATURE FROM THE BLACK LAGOON** and Ponda Baba ("Walrus Man") from **STARS WARS: A NEW HOPE**. For me, I think, the film holds more significance in my memory because a family friend would occasionally set me on his lap and regale me with horrific stories of the bone-eating mole men that lived beneath my home. The film put a face to a name and a lifelong monster movie fan was born.

# HOW I Learned to Love Monsters
### by CT McNeely

For as long as I have loved movies, I have loved action movies. Jean-Claude Van Damme, Arnold Schwarzenegger and their ilk were in the movies that I had on repeat and committed to memory. I had certainly been exposed to other genres and loved cinema in general, but action and martial arts movies were what really did it for me. They still are.

So, as a child, when my dad came home from the local mom-and-pop video rental joint and said he had a Schwarzenegger movie called **PREDATOR** (1987) for us to watch, my mind was immediately ablaze with speculation. I imagined the tagline "Arnold Schwarzenegger is **THE PREDATOR**" printed on a poster of an illustrated Governator, either as a cop who had been *pushed too far* or a one-man army who had to take out all the bad guys and save the day.

I was wrong.

Instead, when the skinned bodies start showing up hanging in the trees, it became apparent that this was a different kind of movie. This was not Sigourney Weaver contending with a xenomorph. It was Arnie. And the alien had already killed the guy who wrote **LETHAL WEAPON** (Shane Black), Jesse "The Body" Ventura, and Carl "Apollo Creed" Weathers! Schwarzenegger was *not* the Predator—he was the prey!

And the Predator was amazing to watch. The alien had a very interesting back-story, only hinted at in the movie (and, in my opinion, almost ruined in the AVP movies later, although I enjoyed the comics that preceded them), and was unnerving to my impressionable young mind. It is an excellent blend of the action movie with touches of horror and science fiction and is one of the best examples of it to date. In his essay for the Criterion DVD release of **THE FRIENDS OF EDDIE COYLE** (1973), Kent Jones says, "Young film fans raised in the multiplex era might look back and lament the fact that no one is making movies like **THE FRIENDS OF EDDIE COYLE** anymore. The truth is that they never did. There's only this one". That applies here too. So many fans talk about how Hollywood doesn't have the balls to pull off things like **PREDATOR** nowadays. Truth is, this one spawned many imitations and a franchise, but both the imitators and the franchise failed to capture the magic again. It all came together for this one.

After this, I have loved to hate many movie monsters. Godzilla, the alien from John Carpenter's **THE THING** (1982), the werewolves from **DOG SOLDIERS** (2002), but I can still remember the feeling **PREDATOR** gave the young version of me. Between you and me, my mind still runs wild with the theories about the alien's origins and the finer details that the movie doesn't tell you. I still like those ideas more than what the sequels and spin-offs came up with.

So yeah, I'm a fan. A big one.

# OUR ENEMY

### by John Walter Szpunar

School days, 1977. Well, not exactly school just yet. By my calculations, I was four years old, going on kindergarten. But somewhere in those weird, dream-like days, I was introduced to my first monsters, and they came to see me every afternoon, courtesy of the fuzzy reception of a small black and white television set in my childhood home.

I don't know how I had control of the TV, but I did. For at least two hours a day, the thing was mine, and I did my best to make use of it accordingly. Earliest memories of those TV screen days: The bizarre and haunting *Johnny Smoke* PSA that must have still been running in the late '70s, another PSA about some Don Quixote-like character who jousted windmills with giant toothbrushes (if *anyone* else remembers this, please get in touch; I'm sure I didn't dream it), and a total indifference to *Mister Rogers' Neighborhood*. Sure, there was *Speed Racer*. Sure, there was *Ultraman*. But nothing could ever hold a candle to the crazy things that aired on WXON TV 20. Especially the show that my friends and I called "Giant Robot".

If I'm not mistaken, the thing was preceded by ancient loops of *Popeye the Sailor* cartoons. I clearly remember the opening and closing doors that served as the credit-crawl, and I certainly remember hearing Olive Oil singing, "I want a clean shaven-man!" time and time again. But once that noise stopped, Takeo Yamashita's Morricone-like opening theme kicked in. Before I knew it, I was lost in a world filled with monsters.

As any self-respecting monster kid from the '70s knows, *Johnny Sokko and His Flying Robot* was the story of a kid named Johnny. While vacationing on a cruise ship, he runs into an older traveler named Jerry Mano. The two shake hands and introduce themselves. "It seems so quiet," says Jerry. "But the quiet sea is dangerous these days. Right in this area, ships have disappeared without a single clue as to how. They must have been attacked and sunk somehow".

As if on cue, the ship is promptly attacked by a giant sea monster named Dracolon. "Johnny!" Jerry

**T**he sounds and images will stay with me forever: A grinding noise—something like rusty and ancient gears suddenly coming to life. The first image on the fuzzy black-and-white screen is of a giant robot. The thing lifts its head, turns, and then its jet engines ignite. The rooftop hatch of some secret place slowly slides open as the AIP logo jitters and then steadies itself in the middle of the screen. Some of the gear-like sounds turn out to be the percussion. Yes indeed, we've got music here, and in an instant the low notes begin to work their way up and down the scale. Then, a howling sound fills the room as the robot raises his arms, looks up to the sky, and takes flight. With that, all hell breaks loose as the scratchy-yet-triumphant score kicks into full-gear.

Time elapsed: Roughly twenty seconds. And things were just beginning.

shouts, "That must be the monster that's been causing all the sinking!" The two of them leap overboard, just as Dracolon strikes again. Within seconds, the ship bursts into flames as our newfound friends struggle to stay afloat in the raging sea.

Johnny and Jerry wake up on an island shore and soon realize that Dracolon isn't their only problem. It seems as if the island is crawling with members of The Gargoyle Gang, a group of nasty humans who look like fascist beatniks with their stylish goatees and sharp brown uniforms. The Gargoyle Gang are the henchmen of Emperor Guillotine, an even nastier creature from outer space. Guillotine's goal: The complete and total conquest of Earth. His weapons of choice: Giant robots and alien monsters.

But Johnny and Jerry have stashed a few cards up their sleeves. Turns out that Jerry Mano is a secret agent from UNICORN—an Earth-based organization of scientists that specializes in keeping the planet safe from…well, just this sort of thing. And he isn't above tossing Johnny a pistol when things get rough.

Before long, our heroes are shooting it out with the Gargoyles and they discover Guillotine's ultimate weapon: A towering robot awaiting activation from its creator, Dr. Lucius Guardian. The Gargoyles had kidnapped Guardian, forcing him to…

Aw, heck. If you're reading this 'zine, you know the story. Guardian betrays his captors and entrusts all control of the robot to Johnny (the means of communication being a voice-activated transmitter hidden in a flip-top wristwatch). Soon, Giant Robot and Dracolon are engaged in an all-out grudge match, but the great sea monster is no match for the forces of good, as Unicorn's new weapon delivers a fatal blow. "Again!" commands Johnny. "Again! Be sure!" The robot swings its arms, cocks its head in defiance, and fires another round of missiles into the monster's hide. Back at headquarters, the UNICORN agents cheer. Dracolon has been defeated. But as Johnny and Jerry fly off in the safety of the robot's arms, Johnny somberly muses, "You know…I think the Gargoyle Gang will try again."

He sure wasn't kidding.

When Johnny and Jerry flew off with that robot, I was right there with them. I'd never seen anything quite like this show before. A kid (named Johnny, no less!) gets to run around fighting bad guys with guns? He alone can control the robot? And he's unsupervised by his parents? Sign me up! I sat in front of the TV set religiously until the series reached its 26th (and final) episode. What a tear-jerker that was! But, I met a lot of friends and monsters along the

way. Much older and wiser now, I still visit them on a regular basis. Why?

It could be nostalgia, but I think it's something more. I can think of plenty of films and comics that I was obsessed with when I was a kid. Only a few of them still hold up today. Something about *Johnny Sokko and His Flying Robot* really hit a nerve with me. The attacking monster always died at the end of each episode. But what of the brains behind the attacks? The villains? The henchmen? They tended to stick around for a while. That said, they weren't impervious to bullets, a creature claw, or atomic breath. A case in point is Spider, a character who seemed destined to ham it up as the leader of the Gargoyle Gang for the entire series. And then, one afternoon, he was obliterated by the menacing monster Scalion. "Spider's through!" said Jerry through clenched teeth. I sat in front of the TV in amazement as Spider's lifeless body slowly melted away.

There were other villains, as well. There was Doctor Botanus, a silver-faced madman with the ability to shed his arms when attacked! There was Fangar, a grotesquely malformed being, complete with a peg-leg, a crutch, and a set of choppers so large that they almost negated the point of having teeth in the first place. And then there was Harlequin—possibly Emperor Guillotine's wisest choice while casting his net for undercover agents. He was the only member of the group that could remotely pass as being

human. But, as tricky and evil as these guys were, they still messed up! And the Emperor didn't take mistakes lightly. I almost felt sorry for them when they pleaded for forgiveness (which they were very rarely afforded).

Another thing I consider is the way the show was shot. Sure there were the usual zooms, rear projection glitches, and obvious miniatures, but you could tell that the team behind the camera was having fun. Candid angles were the order of the day, and at times the camera movement and Dutch tilts elevated the ridiculous proceedings to something somewhat downright arty—that is, if you consider comic book cinematography something to be treasured. I certainly do, and I can now see why the look of the series captivated me so.

And then there was the music. The opening theme has stayed with me for my entire life, but the other bits have stuck around, as well. Combine the jazzy, bass-heavy licks from composer Yamashita with the oversized prop guns, larger-than-life monsters, the crazy villains, pop-art camerawork, and you've got a match made in heaven. When I was four years old (going on kindergarten), I called it "big wheel music", and it was always stuck in

my head as I peddled down the sidewalk imagining that I was hot on the trail of Botanus or some other creature that I had imagined.

Imagination. That is the key.

Crazy monsters destroying everything in sight until they're cut down by the forces of good? Check. Weird, soap opera-like relationships between the Emperor and his minions? You got it. Lazy afternoons in front of the television's black-and-white glow? Certainly. Nostalgia? Sure. Can't argue with that. But there was, and is, something more to it than that.

The sounds and images will stay with me forever: A grinding noise—something like rusty and ancient gears suddenly coming to life. And then, the gates opened.

For what it's worth, this was my introduction to the world of fantastic cinema. A life changer, it was. And my life has been all the richer for it.

Giant Robot fans would do well to invest in the recent Shout! Factory DVD release of *Johnny Sokko and His Flying Robot*, complete with detailed liner notes by author August Ragone.

# MONSTER! #1 MOVIE CHECKLIST

## MONSTER! Public Service posting: Title availability of films reviewed or mentioned in this issue of MONSTER!

**HATYARIN** - currently unavailable to purchase; VHS and VCD are long OOP, but it can be watched on YouTube.

**CHAMUNDA** - currently available to purchase as a VCD (*induna.com* is one source), but it can be watched on You-Tube.

**HORROR EXPRESS** - currently available in numerous formats, thanks to its "public domain" status, but the best version I've seen is the MPI DVD/BR double disk set. A version of it can also be watched at YouTube.

**DEVIL'S EXPRESS** - currently unavailable to purchase except in the grey-market world, but it can be watched on YouTube.

**DEVIL'S FETUS** - currently OOP, but it can be watched on YouTube.

**TRAIN OF THE DEAD** - currently available in the USA as a DVD from Tai Seng, but it can also be watched on YouTube.

**JOHNNY SOKKO AND HIS FLYING ROBOT** - currently available on DVD from Shout! Factory. Numerous episodes, clips and related ephemera can also be found—where else?!—at YouTube. Just type the title into the search box and check out the *dozens* of links that pop up!

**TERROR FROM THE YEAR 5000** - there is an *MST3K* "revamp" (i.e., ruination) of this around (including at YT), which was released on DVD by Rhino Video. Like others of their releases, it presumably includes the unfucked-with original version as well as *MST3K*'s fuck-up. Entitled **EL TERROR DEL AÑO 5.000**, there has also been a Spanish-language Region 2 DVD version released as part of American International video's "*Clásicos de Ciencia-Ficción*" series, which presumably comes with English subs (?). On a related note, I also happened to notice while Googling for this video data that there is a (from what I've heard of them, which isn't much, I'm glad to say) pretty horrible "melodic" metal/alt-rock band who use the film's title as their name, which IMO might much better fit a trashy garage punk or psychobilly act.

**TRACK OF THE MOON BEAST** - formerly available on N. American Beta/VHS tape from Prism Entertainment. It later became available from any number of cheap DVD companies, including on American Home Treasures' 2001 *Classic Creature Movies* disc (triple-billed with likewise rather cruddy, full-frame copies of Bill Malone's **CREATURE** and the '70s TV flick **SNOWBEAST**). At least 4 versions of **MOON BEAST** are up for view at YT, including 2 to be avoided if at all possible from *MST3K*. It's also available from Mill Creek Entertainment (natch!) as part of their 12-film *The Best of the Worst* budget box set. I'd be willing to bet that most of the copies floating around were "mastered" (*ugh!*) from the same source (Prism's VHS maybe?).

**RETURN TO NUKE 'EM HIGH VOL.1** - soon be available on Blu-ray and DVD from Anchor Bay Entertainment.

**THE BEAST WITH 1,000,000 EYES!** - double-billed with **THE PHANTOM FROM 10,000 LEAGUES**, **BEAST** was formerly available on Region 1 DVD as part of MGM/Fox's largely essential "Midnite Movies" series. All I could find from the film at YT are a couple clips, as well as a great trailer which will give potential viewers a taste of what to expect…if they're dumb enough to believe the exaggerated hype!

**PULAU PUTRI** - available for viewing at YouTube, in Indonesian, *sans* any subs. The copy there seems to have been ripped from an old VHS tape (?). It has been released onto VCD in Indonesia by Karyamas Vision, which may have been the source of the YT upload. If you do a search for the title there, it should be the first link to pop up (it was for me, but it might well depend on what browser you use). The copy is fairly decent.

**BLUE DEMON CONTRA LOS CEREBROS INFERNALES** - formerly available on a cheapo All-Region DVD from EastWest video, in Spanish sans any subs. Be forewarned before buying a copy though: two different copies of the same disc reviewed herein were missing the whole end sequence of the film (at least 10m!), so possibly their entire pressing was thus affected (?).

**SEEDING OF A GHOST** - available on Shaw Brothers DVD, with English subs.

**THE OCCUPANT** - there is at least one version of this film broken up into 7 parts at YT, with English subs and dual Chinese audio (Cantonese and Mandarin). It is available on All Region DVD from Fortune Star.

**A BITE OF LOVE** - a trailer is available for view at YT. It was issued on HK DVD as part of the "Legendary Collection", but as of this writing the video's name was unknown. It is not to be confused with a 2006 HK KidCom about a little girl and her cutesy puppy-dog, which was released under the same Anglo title, presumably as some sort of in-joke.

**WIZARD'S CURSE** - under this English title, at least one widescreen version (edited for sexual content) is available for viewing at YT, broken up into 7 parts and *sans* any subs. It was released on HK VCD by Star Entertainment Co., and was at some point distribbed in the USA by World Video & Supply Inc. of SF, CA.

# THE tECHnICaL StUFF:

All reviews and articles written by Tim Paxton unless otherwise noted.

**Timothy Paxton, Editor & Design • Steve Fenton, Editor**
**Tony Strauss, Proof Master**
**Brian Harris, El Publisher de Grand Poobah**

MONSTER! is published monthly. Subscriptions are NOT available. © 2014 Wildside Publishing / Kronos Productions. All rights reserved. No part of this publication may be reproduced, distributed, or transmitted in any form or by any means, including photocopying, recording, or other electronic or mechanical methods, without the prior written permission of the publisher, except in the case of brief quotations embodied in critical reviews and certain other noncommercial uses permitted by copyright law. For permission requests, write to the publisher, addressed "Attention: Permissions Coordinator," at the address below.
Tim Paxton @ Saucerman Site Studios, 26 West Vine Street, Oberlin, OH 44074
kronoscope@oberlin.net
**Volume #1 / Issue #1 / January 2014 / 1st Printing**

# IT'S GOOD TO BE BACK, Y'ALL!

## (...HEY, WAIT A SEC: NO IT'S NOT, IT'S *GRRRREAT* TO BE BACK!!!)

As an Englishman might say, "I'm chuffed as a newt!" Which, roughly translated into North American, means, "I'm pleased as punch!"—*You better believe I am, me mateys!* I must admit that a warm, fuzzy feeling came over me when I first got news last year that Tim "They Call Me MISTER Monster!" P. had reprinted my now near to a quarter-century old (*gulp!*) "Mexi-Monster Meltdown" article—which originally ran in the full-size *MONSTER! INTERNATIONAL* #2 (1992)—in the still relatively recent issue #3 (2013) of Kronos' killer and still ongoing sister publication *Weng's Chop* (major kudos must go out to both Brian H. and Tony S. for continuing to support both these worthy 'zine ventures, BTW!). While I didn't actually contribute to every ish of

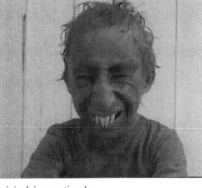

*MONSTER!* digest in its original incarnation by any means (I haven't gone back and checked), I'm pretty sure I had at least one item in all the issues following when I first "got involved" with Tim & Dave T.'s 'zining empire, *circa* 1990-91.

I do believe my first ever contribution to the 'zine was a lengthy ramble about HORRORS OF SPIDER ISLAND, which at that point in time hadn't barely shown its hairy mug since back when it had played first-run, so there was a good deal of buzz about it in trash cinema circles then, hence my write-up. Some of the other titles which spring to mind that I reviewed in what I like to think of as "the little monster" were such '80s/'90s video fodder as THE REJUVENATOR (I gave it a hearty double thumbs-up) and SYNGENOR (two thumbs *waaaay* down!). The first piece I ever wrote for the giant-size *MONSTER! INTERNATIONAL* was a review of the European trash cinema ("ETC") rodent turkey RATMAN. I'm pleased to say I contribbed writings to all of the full-size *M!I* mags, including a lengthy piece called "Of Broads &

Brutes", an article covering vintage monster/horror pulp magazines that ran in the super-slick 'n' glossy *M!I* #4 (which was done as a deluxe split issue with Kronos' titanic T&A zine *Highball*). Hell, I remember that ish even came with a vinyl flexi-disc of prime Man or Astroman? instros too, which provided the ideal soundtrack to read it by. How can you not *love* that shit?! At risk of sounding maudlinly nostalgic here, I just have to say: *"Those were the days!"* ...And they seem to be coming back! A further link with the far-flung past is having Louis *Blood Times* Paul onboard here too.

As well as all the other comparative "noobs" (ya *pups!* ☺) who it's great to have in the posse with us old guns, it'd be great if we can coax a few 'zine scene veterans out of "retirement" to pitch in now and again too, just for old times' sake. When Tim first invited me to contribute new writings to *WC*, I was chuffed enuff. But then when he later asked me to co-edit this long-overdue reincarnation of the massively mighty *MONSTER!* with him, I was immensely touched and flattered on top of it. Not that I'm either a Hindu or a Buddhist, but I can only think of it as karma of the best kind. We can all only hope that this (mostly) all-new incarnation of—dare I say?—*our* zine (meaning ours and yours) lives a long life, and the same goes for its "little" sis, the *'Chop* too.

*MONSTER!*'s back in its old stompin' grounds: best you take care you don't get stepped on, 'cuz this reborn beast's lots bigger and gots even more attitude than it had the first time round! (*Insert terrifying, Godzilla-like ROARRRR here!*)

Here's to yuz, monster mavens...and to *us* too!
~Steve F.

Made in the USA
Lexington, KY
31 March 2015